The Autistic Adult's Toolbox

Real tools for real life—because "just try harder" isn't a strategy

Natalie Diggins

For longer excerpts, full chapter sharing, or other uses, please contact:

Everyday Success Publishing
info@everydaysuccesspublishing.com

Paperback ISBN: 979-8-9985689-0-9
eBook ISBN: 979-8-9985689-1-6
Library of Congress Control Number: 2025907705

www.adultautism.help

Everyday Success Publishing is an independent imprint committed to producing practical, inclusive, and strengths-based resources for autistic adults. We focus on empowering readers with tools that support everyday life in a neurotypical world, with an emphasis on lived experience, accessibility, and clarity.

Book design by Jennifer Stimson

Author photo by Brett Deutsch, Deutsch Photography

If you or someone you know is in crisis or experiencing suicidal thoughts, help is available. In the U.S., you can contact the 988 Suicide & Crisis Lifeline by calling or texting 988, or visit their website for chat support.
Trained professionals are available 24/7.

"To be yourself in a world that is constantly trying to make you something else is the greatest accomplishment."

—Ralph Waldo Emerson

"If you are always trying to be normal, you will never know how amazing you can be."

—Maya Angelou

Welcome

I love my brain.

Sure, at times it can be messy, chaotic, and completely overwhelming, but I wouldn't trade my autistic mind for anything.

My mind can process several different lines of thought at once, making connections and insights quickly. My ears pick up on intricate sound patterns and frequencies that others might miss, such as soft footsteps in a crowded room or the subtle changes in tone during a conversation. I can solve problems with highly creative approaches. And I can perceive and interpret these nuances in ways that add depth and richness to my understanding of the world, giving me a perspective that I deeply value.

For all my struggles—and I do still struggle daily—I embrace the strengths and unique capabilities that come with my autism. They are an integral part of who I am, and they allow me to experience the world in a way that is singularly my own. I don't want or need to be "cured."

I didn't always feel this way. For years, I struggled with frustration, alienation, depression, and meltdowns. But now, in my fifties, I've spent decades developing tools to navigate a neurotypical world—even before I knew I was autistic.

While not perfect, these tools have allowed me to achieve personal fulfillment. I have held executive roles in both tech startups and publicly traded companies, maintained deep and long-term friendships, and enjoyed a strong marriage. **Simply being autistic doesn't automatically mean that I'm unfit to serve in roles or engage in certain activities if I want to.**

That is the point of this book.

In some ways, autism is similar to other aspects of life that require specific tools for success. Can I expect a pastry chef to bake a cake without an oven, or a carpenter to drive nails without a hammer, or a truck driver to drive without a truck?

No.

I wrote this book because the tools I needed to succeed weren't available at the time—so I created them for myself, and now I'm sharing them with you.

There's a reason "spectrum" is included in the term Autism Spectrum Disorder—experiences and needs can vary widely among individuals. For this reason, some of these tools may work for you, some may not, and some may work for you with modifications. My way is one way, but it's not necessarily the right way or the only way. Pick and choose what makes sense for you.

There's a lot of information here. You can read the book from cover to cover, or you can skip around to the chapters that speak most to you. If that feels like too much, perhaps start with a chapter you find particularly interesting, and set a goal of reading one subsection of it each day. And if that still feels like too much, try starting with just a paragraph—or even a few sentences. Baby steps count. Start small, and build from there.

You'll notice that the chapters in this book follow the same structure. That's intentional. I've found that consistent formatting makes information easier to process, reduces cognitive load, and makes it simpler to find what I need when I need it—and I know I'm not alone in that. For many autistic people, predictability and repetition aren't just helpful—they're what make information usable. If the format feels repetitive at times, that's by design.

It's important to recognize that autistic individuals often face higher levels of stress and mental health challenges, which can sometimes lead to consequences like heightened anxiety, depression, and burnout. These are serious issues that require attention and care.

That's why having the right tools matters. The more we understand our needs, the more we can create strategies that support us. This book isn't about changing who you are—it's about giving you the tools to navigate daily interactions and challenges in a way that works for you.

This book is meant to be lived with, not just read.

*If something here resonates, feel free to share it—just tag **@adultautismtools** (on Instagram) or **@adultautismhelp** (on other platforms), or link to the book so others can find it too.*

Author's Note

I am not a doctor, a lawyer, or a financial advisor. I'm not even an expert on autism. I am, however, an expert on my own lived experience as an autistic adult living in a neurotypical world. For professional advice, please consult qualified professionals.

I was formally diagnosed with Autism Spectrum "Disorder" (the quotation marks are mine; I don't subscribe to the assertion that my autism is a disorder to be fixed or pathologized) and alexithymia as an adult.

I had the time, money, and access to pursue thorough evaluations by medical professionals. That access is a privilege—and not a small one. I'm also professionally established, in a long-term partnership, and able to shape many aspects of my environment. I recognize that not everyone shares these advantages.

It's true that many autistic people—especially women, people of color, and those without access to supportive care—go undiagnosed or misdiagnosed. Discrimination, bias, and systemic inequities shape who gets seen, who gets believed, and who receives support. These are complex and deeply rooted issues, and they matter deeply. Others have written powerfully about the larger forces at play. My contribution is more focused: a set of practical tools, drawn from my own life, built from the inside out.

This toolbox is based on my experience and personal insights. I didn't always recognize exactly how I approached certain things until I set out to document them for this book. And in some cases, I didn't know how to do something at all—I had to figure it out. When that happened, I ran experiments on myself—observing what worked, what didn't, and adjusting accordingly.

This approach is how I naturally think and operate in both my personal and professional worlds. If I don't know how to do something, I keep testing different things until I find what works. In another life, I think I'd enjoy being a scientist.

Thank you to those who have provided inspiration, feedback, and support. Any mistakes, omissions, or insensitivities, purely unintentional, are solely my own.

Table of Contents

The Essentials:

How to Build a Sensory Diet That Keeps You Balanced

- Sensory diets are routines designed to balance your sensory input for focus and well-being.
- Start with keeping a sensory journal to track calming and overwhelming inputs.
- Ask close friends or family for patterns you might miss.
- Use your sensory diet to prioritize energy for what matters most.
- Be flexible—reassess and refine your plan as needs change.

How to Build a Sensory Diet That Keeps You Balanced

I'm a creature of habit.

Most mornings, I wake up before the sun, wrapped in soft cotton pajamas, a pot of Japanese sencha green tea steeping nearby. I keep the room dim, reading by the glow of a single lamp—sometimes literary fiction to ease into the day, sometimes technical reading to engage my mind, sometimes an art book for quiet inspiration. Music plays softly in the background, a familiar station I've returned to for years.

This routine isn't just comforting—it's intentional.

For a long time, I thought I was simply drawn to these habits out of personal preference. But when I looked closer, I realized something deeper: every choice I made in the morning was about sensory balance. The texture of my clothes, the warmth of the tea, the quiet lighting—all of it shaped how I felt before stepping into the world.

It turns out, I had built something without knowing it had a name: a sensory diet.

Sensory diets aren't about strict routines or avoiding discomfort at all costs. They're about understanding what helps you feel grounded and focused— and making intentional choices to support that.

Think of a sensory diet as your blueprint for personal balance.

Maybe you already have parts of a sensory diet without realizing it. Maybe there are things you do—certain clothes you wear, environments you seek out, ways you decompress—that help you function at your best. Or maybe you haven't noticed the patterns yet. Either way, learning how to shape your sensory input can make all the difference.

Sensory Diet Basics

So what is a sensory diet? A sensory diet is a personal routine designed to provide the ideal amount of sensory input needed to perform and stay focused for a period of time.

Some people naturally build one over time—gravitating toward soft fabrics, dim lighting, or quiet spaces without realizing why they prefer them. Others need a more structured approach, identifying which sensory experiences calm, energize, or overwhelm them.

What about you? What is your sensory diet?

Assess Your Sensory Needs

A first step in creating a sensory diet plan is to start with a self-assessment.

Ask yourself: When do you feel your best? What environments energize you? What situations leave you drained? What sensory experiences do you seek out, and which do you avoid?

*Ask those closest to you for insights—
they often notice patterns in your sensory
needs that you might overlook.*

In addition to my own observations, I asked others around me to share what they noticed about me. Some of my greatest insights came from the perspectives of those who see me regularly. They often noticed patterns and reactions that I wasn't fully aware of.

I thought I had my sensory preferences figured out—until a friend made an observation.

"Have you noticed that you get snippy every time the TV is on in the background?" she asked. I hadn't. But once she said it, I couldn't unsee it. I started noticing how my mood shifted when the sound was unpredictable or layered over conversation. That one observation changed how I structured my home environment.

Keep a Sensory Journal

Writing things down can help you spot patterns in your sensory experiences. Try tracking:

- **Time of Day:** When do you feel the most and least comfortable? Morning, afternoon, evening?

- **Activities:** What were you doing—reading, working, exercising?

- **Environment:** Home, work, outdoors, or in transit?

- **Sensory Inputs:** What sounds, textures, smells, or lighting were present?

- **Physical Sensations and Emotions:** Did you feel tense, relaxed, anxious, focused?

- **Interactions and Movement:** Were you alone or with others, stationery or moving?

After a few weeks, review your notes. Are there recurring triggers? What sensory experiences helped you feel calmer?

Building Your Sensory Diet Plan

Once you've identified your patterns, you can start making small changes. Here's a sample plan to help get you started. A blank version is included at the end of the chapter for your personal use.

Time of Day	Activity	Environment	Sensory Input	Physical Sensation	Emotional Response	Mitigation Strategies
Morning	Doing laundry	Home	Sound of metal zipper clanging against dryer drum	Tense	Anxious	• Place clothes with metal zippers in a laundry bag or use a dryer ball to cushion the noise. • Perform laundry tasks at a time when other soothing activities can be done simultaneously to counteract the noise. • Use earplugs or headphones with calming music while the dryer is running.
Morning	Dropping children off at school	School	Crowds, noise from other children and parents	Over-stimulated, fatigued	Anxious, over-whelmed	• Arrive early to avoid crowds. Use a drop-off routine to make the process smoother. • Have a calming item in the car for post-drop-off decompression. • Plan a quiet, low-stimulation activity for after drop-off to decompress.

Time of Day	Activity	Environment	Sensory Input	Physical Sensation	Emotional Response	Mitigation Strategies
While at work	Using a touch-screen device while in an open-plan office	Office	Touch feed-back, notifi-cation sounds, strong cologne from co-work-ers	Hand fatigue, irritated skin (from constant touch), headache and nausea (from cologne)	Tactile discomfort, distracted, frustrated	• Use a stylus, screen protector, or haptic gloves to reduce tactile irritation. • Turn off non-essential notifications to minimize distractions. • Use accessibility features like voice commands to reduce touch interaction. • Use a small desk fan, open a window if possible, or keep an essential oil roller nearby for a neutralizing scent.
While at work	Attend-ing a workshop	Office/ conference room	Various sounds (speak-ers, partici-pants), visual stimuli (slides, lights)	Tense	Over-whelmed	• Choose a seat at the edge or back of the room for easier exit if needed. • Take regular breaks to a quiet area to decompress. • Prepare for the workshop by reviewing the agenda and materials ahead of time to reduce surprises.

Time of Day	Activity	Environment	Sensory Input	Physical Sensation	Emotional Response	Mitigation Strategies
After work	Attending a work happy hour	Bar/ restaurant	Loud conversation, music, crowded spaces	Over-stimulated	Withdrawn	• Offer to organize the event and select a quiet, calm location. • Inform the host or a trusted co-worker of your sensory needs. • Choose a quieter spot or a table on the edge of the room. • Limit time spent in the venue to avoid sensory overload. • Inform a close co-worker about your sensory sensitivities and have a plan for an early exit if needed. • Schedule recovery time, which might include a relaxing post-event activity to decompress.

Time of Day	Activity	Environment	Sensory Input	Physical Sensation	Emotional Response	Mitigation Strategies
Evening	Grocery shopping	Supermarket	Bright fluorescent lights, crowded aisles, varied smells (food, cleaning products), loud announcements	Tense, fatigued, headache, irritated	Overwhelmed, anxious, irritable, stressed, uncomfortable	• Shop during off-peak hours and at smaller stores to avoid crowds. • Use sunglasses or a hat with a brim to reduce glare from bright lights. • Bring earplugs or noise-canceling headphones to manage loud noises. • Make a meal plan and shopping list organized by department to minimize time spent in the store. • For strong smells, try breathing through your mouth, using a lightly scented lotion on your wrist to provide a counter-scent, or wearing a mask to filter out overwhelming odors. • Take regular breaks to a quiet corner of the store or outside.
Evening	Watching a movie with family	Living room	Loud volume, sudden noises, bright and flashing lights	Over-stimulated, sensitive to light and sound	Anxious, overwhelmed	• Use subtitles and lower the volume. • Choose movies with less intense visual effects. • Watch in a dimly lit room and wear tinted glasses if necessary. • Keep a blanket or cushion to provide physical comfort.

In hindsight, many of my own strategies were common sense. The hardest part for me was self-awareness, which is why the observations of those close to me were so critical in helping me see the bigger picture.

In one of those conversations, I described my ideal sensory diet to a neuro-typical friend. She mentioned that she also preferred calm, quiet spaces, as many others do, and asked what was so different between us. It was a fair question. I explained that while a loud noise might be irritating to her, for me, it could feel as intense as someone physically slapping me. What might be a minor annoyance for her can be overwhelmingly intense for me.

Negotiate... with Yourself

Another benefit of mitigating negative sensory impacts is that I free myself up to do more of the things I enjoy.

When I visit a quiet and calming restaurant, I can enjoy dinner out with my family for a longer period. However, if the restaurant is loud and chaotic, I may still go, but I won't be able to stay as long, and I will be significantly fatigued afterward, which may prevent me from doing other activities. I only have so much energy, and I try to use it wisely by prioritizing activities and experiences that are important to me.

Your sensory diet gives you the energy to say yes to what you love.

Let's say it's my husband's birthday, and he wants to celebrate with a party, which will likely be very stressful for me. This is a special event, and he does a lot to accommodate me, so I want to try to make it work.

To manage this, I will reduce my sensory intake even further before and after the event to be present during the party while still protecting myself. Additionally, where I have the flexibility, I'll "smooth out" my sensory inputs by not scheduling high-stress activities close to each other, allowing time to recover.

I make a lot of other trade-offs, a sort of negotiating with myself, on more mundane everyday tasks, too. It's more convenient for me to grocery shop at peak times, but if I wait until less busy times when stores are less crowded, I can shop more comfortably and avoid sensory overload. Where I have control, I don't waste my energy on activities that can be managed in a more sensory-friendly way.

What are your non-negotiables? Where can you adjust your environment instead of forcing yourself to endure discomfort?

Be Flexible, Reassess, and Get Back on Track

Even with a successful sensory diet, unexpected changes in life are inevitable. If changes in your environment or routine occur, it's time to re-look at your sensory diet. Regular self-check-ins and openness to new strategies will help you maintain balance. Flexibility ensures your sensory diet continues to meet your needs in a changing world. Solutions will change over time, so don't worry if what worked before isn't working now.

Reflect, reassess, and refine—
your sensory diet evolves with you.

When these signs appear, start by reviewing your sensory journal to pinpoint any changes. Continue with your known calming activities and experiment with new strategies to find what works best. Seek feedback from friends and family for additional insights.

Take small steps and be patient with yourself as you work to regain your balance.

Consult with Professionals

For a more in-depth, rigorous approach to sensory diets, contact a trained occupational therapist who specializes in sensory integration.

Occupational therapists have the expertise to develop personalized sensory diet plans and offer practical strategies for managing sensory input. They can also help you track your progress and make necessary adjustments over time. Additionally, they can provide resources and tools to better understand your sensory preferences and how to accommodate them in different environments.

My Sensory Diet Journey

Your sensory diet isn't about controlling the world around you—it's about giving yourself the best possible experience within it.

I used to think I had to tough it out. That if I just pushed through discomfort, I'd adapt. But that's not how it works. The more I listened to what I actually needed, the easier everything became.

The way you experience the world will change over time, and so will your needs. The strategies that work today might not work forever. The key is flexibility—paying attention to what helps, adjusting when necessary, and recognizing that your comfort and well-being are worth prioritizing.

Trust yourself. You know your needs better than anyone else.

∴ **Tool:** Sensory Diet Planner

Once you understand your sensory patterns, the next step is putting that knowledge into action. This planner helps you map out your daily sensory experiences, identify patterns, and adjust them to maintain balance.

Time of Day	Activity	Environment	Sensory Input	Physical Sensation	Emotional Response	Mitigation Strategies
Morning						

The Essentials:

Managing Shutdowns and Meltdowns

- Shutdowns are expressed inwardly; meltdowns are expressed externally.
- Both are involuntary responses to being overwhelmed—spot early signs to take control.
- These reactions, which I'll call "downs," are not tantrums—they're crises.
- Patterns of stress build slowly—it's rarely one trigger, but many combined.
- Prepare with a Down Plan to reduce intensity of your downs.
- Recovery requires rest and self-compassion—take small, incremental steps.

If any of these points helped you reframe something or feel seen, feel free to share it with someone else—just tag @adultautismtools (on Instagram) or @adultautismhelp (on other platforms), or link to the book so others can find it too.

Managing Shutdowns and Meltdowns: A 3-Phase Action Plan

Wailing sirens, crowded public spaces, and arguments with those I care about—it had been days of sensory overload. It was too much input, and my tools could no longer keep up.

"I can't, I can't, I can't!" I told my husband when he asked what was wrong.

This is coded language in my household, a sort of early hurricane warning system that alerts those around me that I'm spiraling down. I had already stopped forming complete thoughts, and these words were all I could say. A shutdown was imminent.

Shutdowns vs. Meltdowns: What's the Difference?

I normally refer to these episodes as meltdowns, but really, what I usually have are called shutdowns. What is the difference?

Both shutdowns and meltdowns are intense, involuntary responses to overwhelming sensory, emotional, or cognitive inputs. While their underlying cause is the same, they differ in how they manifest.

Shutdowns are *internal*, and as the name implies, they cause the person to withdraw. In my case, I become non-verbal, my eyes glaze over, I move slowly, I become numb, and I might curl into the fetal position. While my involuntary reflexes continue to function, I am otherwise completely shut down.

Shutdowns and meltdowns are the body's way of saying, "Enough!"

Meltdowns, on the other hand, are *external*. While a meltdown may manifest as an explosive reaction—such as yelling, crying, or even aggressive behavior—it's still a result of the same overwhelm that causes a shutdown. It's simply a different outward expression of that internal overload.

A shutdown may follow a meltdown, and a meltdown may follow a shutdown, or either may occur on its own—they aren't mutually exclusive. Both are part of the same spectrum of coping mechanisms requiring their own compassionate approach to support.

What They Aren't

Shutdowns and meltdowns are not tantrums.

They are crises. They are intense, involuntary reactions to feeling over-whelmed when a person's coping mechanisms are inadequate.

To keep things simple, I'll be calling both shutdowns and meltdowns "downs" for the rest of this chapter.

While downs might look like tantrums from the outside, especially in the case of meltdowns due to their outward nature, they are fundamentally different.

In adults:

- Downs are involuntary, while tantrums are typically deliberate.

- Downs are about a loss of control, whereas tantrums are often about testing limits and seeking control.

- Downs are the body's attempt at regulation, whereas tantrums are often resolved once the individual achieves a desired outcome.

- Downs occur with little to no awareness of their surroundings, while tantrums are often driven by a deliberate awareness of how others will respond.

Now that we've sorted out the differences between shutdowns, meltdowns, and tantrums, let's focus on what you can do to manage these experiences before they happen, while they're occurring, and after they're over.

3 Phases for Managing Downs

I wish I could say that it's possible to get to a place where downs never happen, but in my case, at least, that's not likely. Instead, my goals are to reduce the number of downs, minimize their duration when they occur, and improve my recovery time afterward.

To do this, I break the process into three phases, focusing on what I can do in each: the lead-up to a down, the down episode itself, and the recovery immediately after.

1. Go on the Offense

The most frequent advice to manage a down is to prevent it from happening in the first place. If only it were that easy. While there's truth to that advice, of course, it's not always practical or effective depending on circumstances (more on that later). Still, it's a good idea to follow your sensory diet (see the chapter "How to Build a Sensory Diet That Keeps You Balanced" for more information) and try to remove yourself from trigger situations as they occur.

Awareness of the first signs can help you regain control before it escalates.

I find it particularly helpful to identify the patterns that lead to a down. A single trigger may be harder to notice, but when I look at the build-up, both retroactively and after I've recuperated, it often involves a combination of stressors that slowly chipped away at my coping mechanisms. It could be a mix of sensory overload, social interactions, or emotional stress piling up over the course of a day or week. It's not any one trigger—it's the many combined.

Recognizing this cumulative effect can better help you intervene early before a full down occurs, but if that's not successful, you need a plan for what to do when you're in crisis.

2. Create Your Down Plan in Advance

Creating a Down Plan means acknowledging that crises can happen—it's about being prepared to handle them effectively. By knowing in advance how you'll respond when you feel a down approaching, you give yourself the best possible chance of reducing its impact. It's like an insurance policy (you'll notice I build a lot of these into my life). You prepare for the worst while hoping for the best.

Your Down Plan is your safety net: Prepare for the worst, and let it give you peace of mind even if you don't need it.

For me, this means always having an exit plan. If I'm in a loud space, I make sure I know where the nearest quiet room is. If I'm traveling, I pack noise-canceling headphones and a weighted lap pad. I also have pre-written messages on my phone that I can send to my husband when words become too difficult. These small things don't prevent a down from happening, but they make the experience more manageable.

Your Down Plan may look completely different—tailored to your specific needs and triggers. It may include things like safe places to retreat, who to contact for help, items to bring with you, and actions you can take to regain control or at least mitigate the intensity of the experience. The idea is to reduce decision-making when you're at your most vulnerable.

Creating the plan may at first seem like a daunting task, particularly if you struggle with executive function, but there's a nifty, free and online tool called Goblin.tools that will do the heavy lifting for you.

According to their website, Goblin.tools is designed to support neurodivergent individuals with simple, focused tools that help break down complex tasks.

Brilliant.

At the Goblin homepage, simply type something along these lines:

"I need to create a custom shutdown/meltdown plan for when I'm having an autistic crisis. What should I do?"

And Goblin will create a step-by-step, detailed plan that you can further customize. Here's a truncated sample of what the site might suggest:

- Identify early signs of a down (e.g., fatigue, avoidance). Retreat to a quiet space with sensory tools like headphones or a weighted blanket. Practice deep breathing or calming activities. Use visualization techniques to mentally transport yourself to a peaceful space.

- Engage in a calming activity that you find comforting, such as listening to soft music or drawing.

- Reach out to a trusted person for support if you feel safe doing so, or communicate your needs.

- Set boundaries with yourself and others as you transition back into your routine.

- Ask for understanding or accommodations from friends, family, or co-workers as needed.

- Reflect on triggers after the episode to refine your Down Plan.

- Stay connected to a community of people who understand and relate to your experiences.

There are other helpful tools on the site that I encourage you to check out as well, such as the *Judge* (Am I misreading the tone of this?), the *Estimator* (Just tell me how long this is probably gonna take), and the *Compiler* (Compile my braindump into a list of tasks).

Thank you to Bram De Buyser for developing and maintaining Goblin.

3. Recovery

Recovery from a down doesn't happen instantly and is closely tied to the duration and intensity of the episode. It can range from a few hours to several days or longer. I nearly always need at least a night of sleep before I can start to claw my way back to myself, but it can take a few days and even weeks that can segue into burnout if I'm not careful. But really, sleep is my most important recovery tool.

Recovering gently from a down means taking intentional, manageable steps—each one helps restore your strength and balance.

When I'm ready, I continue the recovery process by getting my sensory diet back on track, plus I:

- Give myself permission to experience the down without shame or embarrassment. The down is not a sign of weakness but a reflection of how much I've handled.

- Reduce my workload and schedule, where possible, and allow for extra recharging time to ensure I'm not rushing back into situations that could trigger another down soon.

- Set small, achievable goals for myself. Maybe it's as simple as a five-minute walk each day, and then gradually building up from there.

- Make sure there's at least one thing a day I'm looking forward to. It could be eating a favorite food, listening to new music, or sitting outside for a few moments. Simple pleasures.

- Ask myself, are there any new boundaries I need to set? This could include reassessing commitments, reviewing cumulative triggers, and saying no to activities that drain me.

I don't bounce back to full strength right away, and I've learned to accept and plan for that. What's important is recognizing your needs, being gentle with yourself, and giving yourself the time to heal. It's about building resilience and practicing self-compassion.

Building Confidence for the Future

The more I've learned about managing my downs, the less frequent they've become. After decades, I only have a major shutdown a couple of times a year, and a handful of smaller ones that are easier to manage. But I no longer see them as failures. They are simply part of how my brain processes too much sensory information—a system that sometimes needs a reset, just like anyone else's, even if mine looks different.

I used to fear my downs. Now, I respect them.

Build confidence for the future: fewer downs, shorter durations, and quicker recoveries.

Each one teaches me something—about my limits, about what supports me, about the patterns I need to recognize sooner. The goal has never been to eliminate them entirely but to build a life where they happen less often, last for shorter periods, and don't derail everything. I don't always get it right. But I no longer feel powerless when they happen.

I trust myself to get through them. And that trust is what gives me real control.

⠾ **Tool:** Post-Down Reflection Journal

Use this journal to reflect on a down after it happens. The goal is to identify patterns, assess what worked, and refine your Down Plan for future instances.

1. What triggered the down?

(Think about sensory, emotional, or situational stressors. Was there one specific event or a build-up of triggers?) Example: *Loud noise from construction, lack of sleep, and an overwhelming meeting at work.*

_____

_____

_____

_____

_____

2. What early signs did I notice?

(Reflect on physical, emotional, or cognitive cues that appeared before the full down.) Example: *Feeling shaky, words not coming easily, avoiding eye contact, deep fatigue.*

_____

_____

_____

_____

3. What actions did I take during the down?

(What steps did you try to manage the situation? List what helped and what didn't.)

Example:

- *I put on noise-canceling headphones (helped).*
- *Tried to push through the meeting without a break (didn't help).*

_____

_____

_____

_____

_____

4. What helped me recover afterward?

(List the strategies, tools, or activities that helped you recharge.)
Example:

- *Taking a nap.*
- *Drinking warm tea.*
- *Canceling evening plans to allow more rest.*

_____

_____

_____

_____

5. What can I adjust or refine in my Down Plan?

(What changes can you make to your Down Plan based on this experience?) Example:

- *Schedule 5-minute breaks during intense meetings.*
- *Carry noise-canceling headphones in my work bag at all times.*
- *Ensure I get at least 7 hours of sleep on nights before big tasks.*

_____

_____

_____

_____

_____

_____

6. Self-Compassion Reminder

Write a kind statement to yourself about what you learned and how you handled this situation. Example: *"It's okay that I needed time to recover. I'm learning what I need, and I'm proud of the steps I took."*

_____

_____

_____

_____

_____

Tuning In, Not Out, with Earplugs

When I lived in temperate California, I wore a single proper coat only a few times a year—it was my "winter" coat. After moving to NYC, with its drastically varied climate (bright sunshine, rain, snow, and heavy winds often in the same day), that "winter" coat became my late spring coat. I had to buy a range of coats to get through the seasons, which I now call my quiver—like a quiver of sails, each chosen for different conditions.

As it was with coats, so it became with earplugs. The city was far louder and more unpredictable than I was used to, and I suddenly had access to new experiences not easily available in my former community. My single pair of earplugs was inadequate, leaving me unable to enjoy some social activities and the world around me. Meanwhile, on the positive side, audio technologies were constantly improving.

Following the example of my coats, I built a quiver of earplugs that I now always carry with me to suit a range of conditions and experiences. Now, I never have to miss out because of loud sounds.

My earplugs fall into three main categories: **sound-adaptive**, **general-purpose foam, and high-fidelity**.

1. The AirPods Pro 2 and their **sound-adaptive** management features were a game changer for me (I have no affiliation with Apple; this is my genuine opinion). The AirPods are my workhorses that I wear every day. I primarily use them when I'm having **conversations** in loud spaces, such as restaurants or busy offices.

2. The *Conversation Boost* feature makes it easier to hear someone speaking directly in front of you. It isolates and clarifies it for better understanding. The *Ambient Noise Reduction* feature minimizes background noise, making it less distracting. Taken together, they boost the voice of the person you're speaking with, while simultaneously reducing distracting background sounds for a more focused listening experience.

3. **General-purpose foam earplugs** are designed to block out high volumes of sound without focusing on sound quality. I use them at **sporting events, for dental work, and while reading.** They're inexpensive, so I buy them in bulk and stash extra pairs in purses, coat pockets, gym bags, book bags, and anything else I take with me out and about. They're especially handy

when I need to walk near heavy construction. I can pop them in, walk past the noise, and then put them away for next time.

4. **High-fidelity earplugs** are designed to reduce the overall volume of sound while preserving the clarity and natural quality of music and speech. Unlike standard earplugs, which can muffle or distort sound, high-fidelity earplugs maintain sound clarity but at a lower volume. I find them particularly useful for **concerts** where I want to hear the nuance of the music. At Olivia Rodrigo's concert at Madison Square Garden (yes, I was one of the few people in the arena old enough to legally buy beer), I wore high-fidelity earplugs and could clearly hear her aggressive guitar riffs as well as her quieter, emotionally charged vocals.

Start with a Sound Check

Regardless of which type of earplug I use, putting them in while in a loud environment feels like the sound equivalent of instant pain relief. Because of that, I never hesitate to use them, though they sometimes require a bit of adjustment.

When I use sound-adaptive earplugs, I often speak so softly that the other person can barely hear me. On the other hand, when I wear general-purpose foam earplugs, I'm so loud that not only does my conversational partner hear me, but so does the entire room!

The way I handle this is by doing a "sound check" when I start a conversation. I let the other person know that I'm sensitive to sound and ask if my voice level is comfortable or if I need to adjust how loudly I'm speaking. My friends are used to this now, so I simply say, "Sound check!" and they know what I mean and respond accordingly.

Having the right earplugs isn't about tuning out of what's happening around me. I want to engage with the world, very much so, but I want to do so in a way that's healthy for me.

By carrying a quiver of earplugs (and plenty of backup foam ones), I've found a balance of being in it without being overwhelmed by its sounds.

The Essentials:

My Husband Is an NT and I'm an ND

- *"I want, I need"* language clarifies where compromise is possible and where ND needs are non-negotiable.

- A *no-fighting-dirty* rule protects trust, even during emotional conflicts.

- Balancing ND and NT social needs requires deliberate strategies so that both partners' needs are met.

- In a shared schedule, adding some structured check-ins and routines offers predictability for ND partners while allowing flexibility for NT partners.

- Our differences challenge—and then enable—us to communicate more clearly, connect more deeply, and grow stronger as partners.

My Husband Is an NT, and I'm an ND: How We Make It Work

On the surface, my husband and I couldn't be more different.

My husband is an NT; I'm an ND. He's tall and loud; I'm petite and quiet. He enjoys the frenetic energy of a crowd; I enjoy the calm of being by myself. When he shows love, it's like a pot boiling—exuberant and overflowing with intensity. When I show love, it's more subtle, like a dish of ceviche, cool and contained.

And yet, despite these differences, and many more, we love each other very much. Yes, we have our struggles, but what relationship doesn't? Our challenges may not be typically what couples encounter, but with a few tools, ours works for us.

Relationships, whether ND or NT, start with a strong foundation. Before addressing our unique differences, we built a solid base centered around clear communication, mutual respect, and trust.

Our Foundation

I Want, I Need

The most important element of our foundation is language.

To work through these differences, we've learned the importance of clear communication and compromise through the phrase *I want, I need*.

A want is something desired but not essential for comfort or well-being, allowing room for flexibility or compromise. A need is something essential for well-being or functioning, with little room for compromise.

For example, I may say that I *want* Thai food for dinner. It's a desire, and whether I have Thai cuisine or something else won't adversely impact me.

But I *need* to eat that dinner in a quiet, calm restaurant. If I dine in one that's the opposite, it will undermine my well-being and potentially bring on a down.

Clear communication and trust are the foundation of any relationship—ND and NT alike.

On the other hand, my husband may prefer Italian food. In this case, we might compromise and dine in a calm, quiet Italian restaurant. We both win.

It works the other way around, too. As a child, my husband was mauled by a dog, which left him with an overwhelming fear of them. When we're walking and encounter a dog—no matter how friendly—he needs me to step between them to prevent him from panicking. Since I don't fear dogs, it's not an issue for me.

His panic is his version of a down. While my downs are caused by being on the spectrum, his panic attacks stem from his life experiences. Both are equally valid and require us to compromise for each other's mental well-being.

The phrase *I want, I need* gives us a clear framework for identifying where we can compromise and where we can't. It helps us prioritize and avoid unnecessary conflicts, so we focus on what matters instead of minor issues.

In addition to a language tool, we also have one unbreakable rule for conflict resolution: No matter how intense things get, we never fight dirty.

#1 Relationship Rule

Fighting dirty is when you know your partner's emotional vulnerability, and you use it against them.

- It's telling your partner they're acting like their mother/father/brother/sister or some other person your partner has a charged relationship with.

- It's using hurtful or degrading language aimed at something you know your partner is insecure about, like their job, their appearance, or a past mistake.

- It's bringing up something personal or sensitive that your partner has confided in you, like a fear, an insecurity, or past trauma, just to win the argument.

It's taking the trust your partner has gifted you and weaponizing it against them.

Don't fight dirty.

Building Trust

With the language of "I want, I need" and the rule of not fighting dirty, we've built a foundation based on mutual understanding and respect.

This foundation helps us resolve our differences. I never question my husband's motives—he's shown, time and again, that he only ever wants the best for me, even when we disagree.

Trust also helps us take risks in our relationship. It's why we can suggest new ways of handling challenges or try out each other's solutions, knowing we're both working toward the same goal of making life better for us both. Without trust, it would be much harder to grow and evolve as partners.

Our shared emotional bank account is full. Now, with this bedrock, we're ready for the reality of day-to-day life.

Managing Our Differing Needs

As much as trust and communication strengthen our relationship, daily life still requires us to manage the realities of our individual needs. Whether it's how we socialize, manage our communication styles, respond to routine, or handle sensory input, our approaches often diverge. But with a bit of thought and flexibility where each of us is able, we've learned to find common ground.

Managing Differing Social Needs

I already know how to balance my own social needs, but it becomes more challenging in a relationship when the needs of a second person are involved.

Social strategies like drop-bys, couple time, and quiet time for recovery balance our differing needs.

My husband loves being around people; it gives him energy. Me, I prefer being by myself, and when I am around people, it's draining. To manage, we've developed socializing tactics:

- **I attend joint social engagements that we jokingly call "command performances."** This is our lighthearted way of prioritizing the most important social functions. The idea came about early in our relationship, when my husband asked me to join him on nearly every social occasion, not realizing how draining it was for me. He thought I was like him and would enjoy the interaction.

- **Deploy the drop-by strategy.** Command performances are few and far between, but when they do occur, we might use the drop-by strategy. Ahead of the event, we identify the people who are most important to us. My husband will then arrive at the event before I do, I drop by to make an appearance and participate, I actively seek out and greet those already pre-identified, and then I leave while he stays and enjoys himself.

- **Use the meet-up strategy.** My husband might attend a social gathering on his own, and then we meet up afterward. For example, he'll often grab a drink with a colleague or group after work, and then we'll meet up later at dinner.

- **We schedule alone time for me, while my husband goes out and socializes on his own.** To stay emotionally connected, we have a practice where, if one of us is socializing without the other or traveling, the first one to go to bed texts the other goodnight, and in the case of travel, the first one awake texts the other good morning.

With these tactics for social engagement, my husband's needs are met, we as a couple maintain a connection, and my need for quiet alone time is respected.

Managing Differing Communication Needs

Some people believe that autistic people can't lie. I don't know if that's true or not, but in my case, it's that I don't know I'm supposed to; I lack a filter. If my husband asks me for my opinion—on his outfit, a decision he's made, or how he's handling a situation—I give him my honest answer, without sugarcoating.

This can be especially challenging when dealing with emotionally fraught issues. I mean no hurt or harm, but sometimes my directness can come off as blunt or insensitive, especially if he's expecting a more supportive or gentle response.

At the same time, I sometimes struggle to understand his emotions or even my own. It took me a long time to realize that my difficulty naming my emotions wasn't just a personal quirk—it's actually a common trait among autistic people. It has a name: alexithymia. It means I don't always recognize or articulate what I'm feeling right away, even when those feelings are strong.

It's not just that NTs don't always get me—I don't always get them either. That's what researchers call the "double empathy problem." Basically, it's a two-way street: NTs and NDs each have their own ways of communicating, and misunderstandings happen because we see things so differently.

Recognizing this difference has been important for both me and my husband. It helps me be more intentional in expressing what I feel, and it helps my husband understand that my seeming lack of emotion doesn't mean I don't care—it's just harder for me to articulate or even identify what I'm feeling in the moment.

When dealing with sensitive topics, I apply a temporary filter while my husband engages in emotional reflection.

My temporary filter focuses on gentle framing and reassurance. Depending on the situation, I might start a difficult conversation with a script like, "I know you didn't mean to, but…" or "I love you, and we're okay," and then follow it with what comes naturally for me: direct feedback. This allows me to be honest while showing my intent isn't to wound. It keeps the conversation open and lets my husband know that even when I'm being direct, my support is constant.

In return, my husband engages in emotional reflection, which comes naturally for him but can be difficult when he's feeling vulnerable. When he feels hurt by my words, rather than reacting, he responds with, "Here's how what you said made me feel…" This helps us keep the conversation productive and prevents misunderstandings from escalating into an argument.

You might wonder why I don't install a "permanent" filter if I'm able to use one temporarily.

For me, it's a form of masking—suppressing or modifying traits to appear more neurotypical—which I try to limit. I focus my energy on using the filter during important discussions, especially when doing so ensures I won't hurt others. But for everyday interactions—especially on unimportant topics—it's too exhausting to maintain constantly.

Managing Differing Routine and Flexibility Needs

I find comfort in predictability, and sudden changes in routine can cause me distress. I rely heavily on mentally preparing in advance for new activities. My husband enjoys spontaneity and adapts easily to changes. If left on his own, he rarely plans and prefers ambiguity.

I like to visualize how we balance our differing needs:

As a couple, our day is like the outline of a box, with clear boundaries. Within that box, my day is likely highly structured, while my husband's stays more fluid. The perimeter is where our styles meet and where we have common structure.

Practically, we accomplish this by having a daily "stand-up" meeting—similar to a quick check-in at work—where we review our schedules, any tasks we need from each other, changes to our usual routines, and what we might have for dinner. The most important topic is where our schedules intersect.

This helps set expectations and keeps things predictable for me while giving my husband the flexibility he needs. If plans change throughout the day, as they often do, one of us will text the other—we avoid surprises.

Truth be told, my spontaneous husband not-so-secretly has come to appreciate having some structure in his life. He now gets to go to that sold-out show (because his wife got tickets in advance), he's more productive (thanks to our daily stand-up meetings that keep him on track), and we avoid unnecessary conflicts (since the important things are discussed and planned ahead).

*With trust and thoughtful strategies,
our differences become strengths—
not barriers to connection.*

Managing Differing Sensory Needs

Managing our differing sensory needs (really, they're my sensory needs) is one of the most challenging and frequent issues we face in our relationship. We make it work mostly through compromise and scheduling, and the best way to explain how is through real-life examples.

- My husband enjoys playing music at full volume. We compromise by agreeing that he can listen as loudly as he likes (as long as it doesn't disturb the neighbors) when I'm not home. As I make my way back, I text him, and he lowers the music before I arrive.

- The sound of dishes being unloaded from the dishwasher, especially during quiet times, is jarring for me. We've agreed that my husband will unload the dishwasher when I'm in the shower, and in exchange, I make the bed, which is something he doesn't enjoy doing.

- The sound of our washer and dryer carries throughout our home—there's no escaping the noise. So, we've worked out a system: We run them when I'm about to leave the house.

- Movements in my peripheral vision can overstimulate me—whether it's my husband pacing while talking on the phone or bouncing his foot. To manage this, we've agreed that if he needs to pace or move around, he'll do it in a different room from me. To avoid arguments, we use a simple code word: "movement." This lets my husband know what's bothering me, signals that one of us needs to change rooms (first person in the room gets it), and prevents a fight from starting.

Stronger Because of, Not Despite, Our Differences

I believe our relationship works not despite our differences but because we've embraced them.

Our differences push us to communicate more, be more thoughtful, and challenge assumptions. And while it's not always easy, these very differences strengthen our bond. In navigating (and sometimes stumbling over) our challenges, we've built a deeper trust and respect for each other.

ND or NT, the goal is the same— making life better for each other.

Once I shared with my husband that I'm autistic, it led to a better understanding between us. Now, when I ask him to be quieter, he no longer takes it as a personal attack. I'm not judging him. Quiet environments aren't just a preference for me—they're what I need and how I'm wired.

We may not approach our relationship like other couples, but it feels true to who we are as individuals and partners. We're still figuring things out, but we're growing together and getting better every day.

Interview with
My NT Husband

This interview has been edited for clarity and flow.

Natalie: Thanks for agreeing to talk publicly about our relationship. Are you nervous?

Husband: Not at all.

Well, that makes one of us. Let's dive in. When we first got together, you didn't know that I was autistic. What were your first impressions of me?

Well, you were certainly very different than anybody else I'd ever met. You were completely logical, unemotional, and organized beyond any standard I was ever aware of. You were, of course, hot.

You know I'm going to edit that last part out. (Note: I was overruled.)

And you were deliberate in everything you did. Nothing is left to chance; nothing is left unplanned. It took some getting used to.

That's fairly accurate. How would you describe your own approach to life, and specifically, to relationships?

It's a good question. I would say up until that point, I was more reactionary and less proactive. I also planned a lot less. As far as relationships go, I would say I led more with emotion and less with reason.

In my previous long-term relationship, I was the less emotional one by far, though I was still very emotional. It was new for me to have that world flipped.

I remember one time, but I forget the exact details, when I reacted in a certain way, and you basically said, "You get to do that once, but that's not how we do our relationship." I'm like, wait, that's not how we do this? I thought that's how you did it. I learned a lot about how to have a better and stronger and more respectful and less volatile relationship from you.

I think I know the instance, and it was our first big argument. You sort of exploded. That's when I came up with the "never fight dirty" rule.

This brings up how we engage in relationships differently. How would you say that we each do so based on our individual neurotypes?

One thing jumps out immediately.

If we do have a fight or a difficult discussion, the fight helps me work through whatever I'm feeling and whatever is happening between us. Having the discussion is not at all helpful to you unless there's agreed action at the end of it. You want it to end with a series of steps that will be taken so that the argument doesn't happen again.

And I view life as a series of these things. You can't keep them from happening, but you make them fewer and further between, you make them less volatile, you manage them better. But the goal of essentially eliminating conflict is new to me. Since I don't believe it's possible, I don't spend a lot of time worrying about it.

I wouldn't say that I am trying to eliminate conflict, although I wish I could— I'm more pragmatic than that.

I feel we're aligned on the outcome—a supportive, loving relationship—but how we get there is different. Talking about the issues makes you feel better, almost like a pressure release valve that lets off steam. It drives me nuts to keep having the same fights repeatedly—it's like the movie Groundhog Day where the same day repeats over and over.

If I go through the anguish and the emotion of having the conflict, I expect things to improve, and the only way in my mind things improve is if we agree to outcomes and to do things differently the next time.

Earlier, you said that you hadn't met anyone like me before, but I know you've had other experiences with autistic people. How has your perspective on autism changed since we met, if it has?

The first autistic person that I knowingly talked to was Temple Grandin, the academic and ethologist who gave a TED Talk about autism. I learned from her that someone can have autism and be highly functional. Before that, what I knew about autism I learned from watching Dustin Hoffman in the movie Rain Man.

Then, a friend's child was diagnosed with autism, and it gave me another example of what it can look like. All these people experience autism in different ways, and it validates why ASD is called a spectrum—autism doesn't look any one way.

What I've learned from you is how difficult it is for people with autism to live in a world designed for neurotypicals. Every day I watch you and see how hard it is. I appreciate it, although I won't ever truly know how hard it is because I haven't lived it.

Thanks for recognizing that and for not trying to "fix me."

I'm very blunt, and I approach life in a scientific manner. Despite meaning no harm, I sometimes hurt your feelings. How do you handle situations where I'm too direct and analytical for your comfort?

I cry.

I know you do, and I'm sorry to put you through that. It guts me when I hurt you, and I've been trying to give you reassurance before saying what I think, but I know I don't always get it right.

I mean, it's hard. If I didn't respect you, I wouldn't care what you said, but I do respect you, and sometimes I disagree with you, but even if I do, I still respect you. I don't ever want someone who I love to feel that I failed them.

Here's a fundamental difference between us: If I'm giving feedback on you, me, or us, it's not an indictment of you, me, or our relationship. I know that we're not perfect, and I just want to be better. I can see that I've wounded you with my words, but because they weren't meant or said harshly, I don't understand why I've done so—I'm at a loss.

I look at both my intention and what I perceive to be a lot of hard work to accommodate you. Making your life easier is a big part of my everyday living. And when it's not done right, or it just didn't work, or whatever it is, it's hard on me. It's like the guy who goes up to bat at the World Series with bases loaded and strikes out. I mean, it's just that feeling that I stepped up and took my shot and I failed.

You bring up the accommodations that you make for my autism, and I very much appreciate all the things that you do for me. One reason I think our relationship works is that you also appreciate the things I do for you.

Even if we were both NTs, which we're not, we would be making accommodations for each other. The difference for us is that the accommodations you make for me are due to the way my brain is wired, whereas the accommodations I make for you are related to your life experiences. An example I use in the chapter on NT/ND romantic relationships is your fear of dogs and how I help you manage that. And that's a common thread throughout this book. We're all making accommodations in life, regardless of neurotype.

I agree.

What's something you've learned about yourself and our relationship, especially regarding how you handle differences?

I can manage life in general much better. I think that it's partly age and experience, but it's partly being with you and being in our relationship. I can take myself out of a situation better than I used to be able to, and I'm better able to depersonalize conflict. An example is if I get rejected professionally, I don't take it personally at all. I can be a bit more philosophical.

What is something you think we do better as a couple because of our differing neurotypes?

Each of us optimizes for different things, and each of us recognizes that the thing the other one optimizes for is worthy of doing. In the end, I think we end up having a better life because we balance each other. It would be boring if we were too similar.

Speaking of balance, balancing our sometimes contradictory needs is a big part of how we manage our relationship and lives. How do you make sure your needs are met while also considering my neurodivergent needs?

Early in our relationship, you taught me that you have to be a strong me to be a strong we. At first, I wasn't good at that, and then, over time I learned not to worry when you were being a strong me and I wasn't included. Now, I don't mind going to social events on my own if you want a night off or if you want to do something on your own. It took time, but I feel we do this well. It's probably because we're secure in our relationship.

I want to talk about something that's particularly challenging for me—my downs. While I've been able to manage my downs better as I age, they still happen. A few months ago, I had a major down, one of my worst ever. It took me weeks to recover. I know my downs don't just affect me but you as well. How do you approach navigating my downs as my partner?

I think the most challenging thing is to understand that at times there's nothing I can do to help. Certainly, if it's because of something I've done, I can cease the behavior. Or if it's a situation that's problematic for you, I can help to remove you from it, and then there are times where I'm not aware of what's going on. The downs are mysterious, and I really don't know what to do.

I think something you've done a great job with is anticipating crowds and what they do to me. If we must move through a crowd, which unfortunately is often, you sort of get a bubble going around me and try to find a path through the crowd for us that is less dense. I really appreciate that.

You see me in great anguish and distress when I'm in a down. How do you cope or manage your own emotions?

In the moment, I try to manage it. Managing crises is something I do in my job, and it's something I've done over my life with close family members who have various kinds of emotional and non-neurotypical reactions. And so being around that has allowed me to at least in the moment manage the situation and not make it personal.

What do you think we could do together to make these times less stressful for both of us?

The thing to do is to better anticipate the potential for downs. So, for instance, we recently decided to go to a big event, and before we bought tickets to the event, I looked at it and realized that it was going to be tough for you. We talked about what might happen, things we could do to mitigate problems, and then together we decided that based on all of that, the experience of the event was worth the risk. It was helpful that we had the conversation prior to attending so that we could be deliberate in our approach and prepared for what might happen. In the end, everything went well, and we had a good time.

I appreciate how you take the time to think through situations with me like that—it makes a big difference. Speaking of challenges...What are some of the most difficult things about being with me as someone on the spectrum?

I would say the most challenging thing is when we have plans, and some really awesome possibility comes up for a plan B, but because plan A exists, plan B is just rejected, especially if plan B comes up at the last minute. I understand we're prioritizing your mental health, but we live in New York City, and there's always something interesting happening. I do get FOMO.

I remember early on in our relationship, I would bring up issues I was having because I was on the spectrum and was surprised by your pushback. I might say something—music, a door closing, the heater running—was too loud for me, and you reacted almost as if I offended you personally.

One day, after the front door slammed on our way out of the house, I winced, and you thought I was being melodramatic. I explained that when the door slammed, it felt like I was being physically slapped. You stood there, looking shocked, and I felt like in that moment you understood. Since then, I try to describe what I'm going through in terms that I think you may be able to understand. For example, when I'm feeling overwhelmed before a down, I may say that it feels like a giant hand is squeezing my heart.

Certainly, that was a telling moment. I think that part of the challenge I was having is that, in my mind, you present as unemotional, and you don't react. And then certain things would happen and you would react very strongly to them, and that was inconsistent to me. I didn't know how to process that. Since then, I've learned that a strong reaction to noise, or a strong reaction to a physical environment, or a strong reaction to crowds provokes what appears as an emotional reaction in someone who I would generally describe as unemotional.

That makes sense—I can see how I may present as contradictory.

What advice would you give to other neurotypicals who are in a relationship with someone who is neurodiverse?

It was incredibly useful to me to access therapy. I learned to better understand how you're wired and to not have anxiety if you reacted in ways that were counter to what I expected. It helped me understand your sensory issues, why you sometimes lack a filter, your discomfort with certain types of socializing, and why you're less emotional.

I learned to take what you say in the spirit with which it was said, and to tell myself, that's just how she communicates.

On the flipside, I think about all the things you do for me, including your willingness to endure loud places and to socialize more. I realize that it's your way of showing love and that you're not about to break up with me. When you share what you're thinking in an unfiltered way, you're not criticizing me; you're sending me a message of how you want to make things better between us, and I need to take it in that spirit.

Anything else you'd like to add?

Yes. If you can understand where your neurodivergent partner is coming from and how the world affects them, and you can take yourself out of that, which is not always easy, but if you can do that and at the same time focus on the amazingness that comes into your life by being with someone who is on the spectrum, it's like you won the lottery.

This feels like a super intense therapy session.

I love you, sweetie.

I love you too, sweetie.

∴ **Tool:** I Want, I Need Worksheet

This worksheet helps you and your partner clarify your wants and needs in specific situations, identify areas for compromise, and find solutions that respect both partners' well-being.

Situation/Topic	Briefly describe the situation (e.g., planning a dinner, managing social events, balancing alone time)
My Want	What I'd like but I can compromise on
My Need	What I absolutely require for my comfort, functioning, or well-being
Partner's Want	Your partner's preference that leaves room for flexibility
Partner's Need	What you partner requires to feel comfortable or secure
Compromise Solution	Brainstorm how you can meet both needs while still allowing for flexibility

EXAMPLE

Situation/Topic	Weekend Plans
My Want	To stay home and relax with a quiet activity like reading or a movie.
My Need	A calm, low-stimulation environment to recharge after a busy week.
Partner's Want	To go out for a spontaneous day trip with friends.
Partner's Need	Time to connect socially and enjoy an engaging, energizing experience.
Compromise Solution	We split the day: My husband goes on the trip in the morning while I recharge at home. We reconnect in the evening with a quiet dinner together.

YOUR TURN

Situation/Topic	
My Want	
My Need	
Partner's Want	
Partner's Need	
Compromise Solution	

Situation/Topic	
My Want	
My Need	
Partner's Want	
Partner's Need	
Compromise Solution	

The Essentials:

Building Friendships That Work for You (and Your Friends)

- Manage differing communication styles and expectations by using consent-based questions like, "Is this the type of feedback you're looking for?"

- Use practical tools like the "Helped, Hugged, or Heard?" question to build mutual understanding.

- Ask yourself how a friendship makes you feel—energized or drained—and use those feelings to guide your next steps.

- Find friendship role models who can inspire you on how to connect with others.

- Not all friendships last, and that's okay—they can still teach valuable lessons to guide your next ones.

- Friendship goes both ways—be the kind of friend you hope to have.

Building Friendships That Work for You (and Your Friends)

I've been described by friends, sometimes on the same day, in contradictory terms:

Thoughtful/Inconsiderate

Generous/Selfish

Polite/Rude

Caring/Uncaring

Genuine/Inauthentic

It's all so confusing.

What kind of person and friend am I, really? I don't feel inconsiderate, or selfish, or rude, or uncaring, or inauthentic, or at least that's not my intention, and yet when viewed through a neurotypical lens, I can see why I may come across that way, even if that's not who I believe I am.

At times, my friends are just as baffled by me as I am by them.

Managing the Disconnect

This disconnect largely comes from the differences in how neurotypical and neurodivergent people interpret social interactions and behaviors. I may mean one thing, but I recognize that the way I express it doesn't always align with a neurotypical way of expressing and acting on the same idea, and vice versa, particularly around communication style, attention to detail, and my focus on boundaries.

I find that it isn't just my style or behavior that is off-putting but that it comes as a surprise; it's unexpected. This is usually when negative traits are attributed to me. Maybe it's a surprise because of my gender, or my age, or how I present socially, or some combination of these factors.

I don't change who I am, but I've learned to be upfront about my communication style and behaviors.

- If asked for my opinion on a topic, I often first respond by saying, "I'm a direct person. Is that the type of feedback you're looking for?"

- If I'm asked to co-host an event, I usually respond with, "I have a high attention to detail; will that work with your organizational style?"

- If a friend invites me to socialize during a busy time, I'll say something like, "I'd love to join, but I need some quiet time to recharge. Can we plan to get together another week instead?"

Directness can be a strength when paired with clear, consent-based communication.

I try to turn what some might see as a liability—like my bluntness—into an asset by leading with clear, consent-based communication. While this is direct, the feedback I've received is that my friends appreciate my effort to meet their needs, in addition to my own.

As people get to know me better and they move from acquaintance to friend, they learn that I'm the person to go to for help and consistency, but not necessarily for emotional support. It's not that I don't want to support my friends emotionally (I do!); it's that I can't provide the kind of support they need. But even to get to that stage of friendship, there usually needs to be a baseline compatibility in our values and personalities.

- **Friend Essentials**

Most people have certain core traits they look for in friends, either implicitly or explicitly. Some of these form a general baseline—honesty, ethics, trustworthiness—but I also have some that are specific to me because I'm on the spectrum. I tend to match well with people who are:

- **Flexible**

People who are flexible can support me in areas where I'm less adaptable. In turn, I hope I offer them something they need, which often, in my case, is structure. It's the "opposites attract" principle in action—where their adaptability balances my need for structure, and we shore up each other's gaps.

- **Consistent**

People who do what they say when they say they'll do it. If someone changes plans frequently or doesn't follow through, I don't want to torture myself wondering if I did something to cause it.

- **Willing to Learn**

People who are open to understanding autism and learning about my needs help me feel accepted and valued.

- **Respectful of Boundaries**

People who respect my boundaries (related to sensory preferences, socializing, etc.) and don't interpret them as criticism of their own choices.

Understanding your needs is just as important as respecting those of your friends.

Understanding what I need for a healthy friendship sets me up for deeper, more fulfilling relationships. But knowing what I need is only half the equation—I also need to know how to build those connections. That's where practical strategies come in.

3 Techniques for Establishing Friendships

Conventional wisdom says that a good way to make friends is to engage in activities to find people with common interests. It's wisdom for a reason—it works. That, plus having an activity to do together takes the stress off other aspects of building friendships, such as making small talk. What can be more challenging is how to engage with those potential friends once you find them. Here are three techniques that work for me:

#1 The Phone Trick

When meeting someone new and hoping to connect later, I used to ask for their contact information and follow up immediately with suggestions for specific plans, dates, and times. Often, I wouldn't get a response, and I couldn't understand why. Later, I realized that sometimes people were just being polite when giving their contact information.

Now, instead of just asking for someone's email (which I prefer because it doesn't require an immediate response), I type a quick, casual message on my phone while they watch, something like this:

Hi Alexis-

I loved meeting and chatting with you at Sean's dinner tonight! Let's connect again soon.

Warmly, Natalie

The next morning, they find an email from me in their inbox. They might not reply, and that's okay because I've kept my effort minimal and have let go of any expectations. But if they do respond, it shows a genuine interest in getting together. That small act of them having to respond to initiate the next steps makes all the difference.

#2 The Pressure Meter

I can come across too strongly with potential friends. I may misunderstand their level of interest and, thinking I'm responding in kind, I end up pushing them away by flooding them with too much attention or enthusiasm.

I use the concept of a pressure gauge to keep in balance. I visualize our interaction as if I'm reading a pressure meter. If my friend is applying in their response, say, 5 lbs of pressure, I try to match that same level of intensity. If I sense that the "pressure" is rising—by me engaging too much or too quickly—I adjust by stepping back. The same goes for when I might start a conversation with, say, 6 lbs of pressure, and they respond more subdued, with a 3. Then, I may dial back my energy to keep the interaction better balanced.

I imagine that this energy dance, for some, is an involuntary reflex. Over time, it's become that for me, too—I don't have to think much about it. The pressure meter served (and still serves) as a training tool.

#3 The "Do You Want to Be Helped, Hugged, or Heard?" Shortcut

My instinct when someone presents me with a problem is to try and solve it, but it's not necessarily what that person needs. Sometimes, they simply want to be heard. Or maybe, they need a hug.

> *Your friends may not need fixing—*
> *sometimes, they just need to be heard.*

Rather than trying to guess what someone needs, I ask, "Do you want to be helped, hugged, or heard?" Most of the time, people's needs fit neatly into one of these three categories. This approach (which my husband and I also use) removes the guesswork in supporting friends and communicates what would be most comforting or useful in the moment.

Having said that, I do hope they choose "helped," as that's where I'm most effective. I am who I am, but this approach reminds me that sometimes the best support is being present in the way friends need most.

Even with the best of intentions, some friendships may reveal warning signs—on both sides—that they're not meant to last. That's where my Friend Flag Tests come in.

How to Spot Friendship Flags

Friendships don't always work out. It's not about one person being bad and the other good; it's more often that the personalities aren't a fit. It can be hard to assess if that's the case, though.

When a friendship starts to feel a bit shaky, I pause and ask myself these questions:

- How do I feel when I think about seeing this person?
- How do I feel when I'm with this person?
- How do I feel after I've seen this person?

We all have bad days. I don't fret if I feel uneasy about my relationship with a particular friend over a few interactions, but as they build up, I do think of those as orange flags; I need to pay attention. If those orange flags continue adding up and create a trend, we're in red flag zone. It's time for me to re-examine the relationship.

> *Ask yourself: Do you feel energized or drained by your friendships?*

Of course, it's not all red flags! There are those "green flag" moments, like when I feel excited to see someone and genuinely enjoy spending time with them. These are relationships worth nurturing and putting extra effort into.

Just as I evaluate friendships for flags, I work on how I can be a better friend myself. That's where my friend Kim comes in—she's the embodiment of green flags.

Find a Friend Role Model

If I wanted to have good friends, I also had to learn how to be one. We all have role models in religion, business, sports, the arts, culture, and other areas of life, yet we rarely have them in friendship. The issue is compounded for me because I may miss the social cues often needed to form healthy friendships.

In my twenties, I met Kim when we both volunteered for Planned Parenthood. She's smart, kind, fun, and she has the biggest heart. She has dear friends today, and not just a few, that she's known since they were in elementary school together. You don't make and maintain quality friendships over decades without being a good friend yourself. She's my friend role model.

Even though we now live thousands of miles apart, Kim is with me all the time.

There's a Christian saying, "What would Jesus do?" It's meant to encourage people to reflect on their actions and think about how they can respond with compassion, empathy, and integrity. My friend version of that saying is, "What would Kim do?"

If confronted with a social situation and I don't know what to do—which is often—I channel Kim. I try to respond in ways that I think correspond with her actions and how she makes me and other people feel valued as her friend. In fact, she's the one who taught me the phrase, "Do you want to be helped, hugged, or heard?"

Find your Kim—or better yet, your Kims, plural. No one person will be all of the things you need. Think about the people who embody qualities you admire, and then learn from their example.

What Friendships Have Taught Me

Not every friendship is meant to last—and that's okay. Sometimes, it's just a matter of personalities not clicking, or a change in circumstances, not anyone doing something wrong. This isn't a reflection of anyone's worth—it's simply a reminder that not all relationships are meant to endure.

Building meaningful friendships takes patience and practice. By recognizing red flags, you can avoid friendships that drain you, while letting green flags guide you toward people who enrich your life.

And while I've managed to build friendships over time—largely by trial and error and with help from the tools I've shared—I recognize that even with them, friendship may still feel painful or difficult for some, especially those under intense life pressure or carrying past social pain. If that's you, please know that struggling with friendship doesn't mean you're doing anything wrong. Friendship isn't a test you're failing. It likely means the conditions around you aren't supporting the kind of connection you need—and that's not your fault.

Every friendship teaches you something—even, and especially, the ones that don't last.

Through it all, I remind myself: Being a good friend is as important as finding one. It's hard work, but when you find friends who match your energy and values, the effort feels absolutely worth it.

∴ **Tool:** Friendship Support Pack

- Friendship Self-Assessment
- Friend Role Model Worksheet
- Friendship Compatibility Checklist
- Friendship Action Plan

Friendship Self-Assessment

Purpose: A guided reflection to help you evaluate the current state of your friendships and identify areas for growth, balance, and mutual understanding.

Instructions: Reflect on the following questions. Write your answers or think them through, focusing on patterns and actionable insights.

1. **What do I value most in a friendship?** Identify the traits or qualities that are most important to you in a meaningful relationship.

_____

_____

_____

_____

2. **Which friendships feel energizing, and why?** Reflect on the friendships that leave you feeling uplifted, respected, supported, or happy.

_____

_____

_____

_____

3. **Which friendships feel draining, and why?** Consider which relationships feel like they take more from you than they give and explore the possible reasons.

_____

_____

_____

_____

4. **Are there specific actions I can take to improve these relationships?** Think about steps you can take to strengthen connections or address issues within these friendships.

_____

_____

_____

_____

5. **What boundaries, if any, do I need to establish or reinforce?** Reflect on where you might need clearer boundaries to protect your well-being and improve your relationships.

_____

_____

_____

_____

6. **Am I giving as much as I'm receiving in my friendships? Do I feel that my efforts are being reciprocated?** Assess whether the give-and-take in your friendships feels equitable and satisfying.

_____

_____

_____

_____

7. **Do my friends understand and respect my neurodivergent needs, or do they want to learn?** Consider how well your friends accommodate your needs and whether there are opportunities for better communication.

_____

_____

_____

_____

8. **What have my friends done that made me feel supported and valued as a neurodivergent person?** Reflect on specific actions, words, or behaviors from your friends that have helped you feel understood and accepted. Use these examples as a guide to identify what support looks like for you, and consider sharing these stories with other friends who may want to support you but might not know how.

_____

_____

_____

Tip: If it feels right, share your gratitude with those friends. They may not realize the impact they've had, and expressing your appreciation could mean a lot to them.

9. **How can I support my friends, especially those wired differently, while balancing my own needs and boundaries?** Reflect on ways to align your support with your friends' needs while protecting your well-being. Consider asking them directly how you can be a better support. Think about what compromises feel comfortable and sustainable for you.

_____

_____

_____

_____

10. **Are there friendships I've been neglecting that I want to invest more time in?** Reflect on relationships that may need more of your attention and how you can nurture them.

_____

_____

_____

_____

Friend Role Model Worksheet

Purpose: A short exercise to identify role models in friendship and what you can learn from them.

Instructions: Use this worksheet to reflect on who inspires you in your friendships and how you can embody their qualities.

Identify Your Friendship Role Models

- *Who in my life embodies the qualities I value in a friend? (List one or more people who inspire you as role models in friendship.)*

_____

_____

_____

_____

Explore Their Actions and Habits *What specific actions or habits make them a great friend?*

- *Do they communicate clearly?*
- *Are they consistent in their actions?*
- *Do they respect boundaries?*
- *How do they show kindness, flexibility, or support?*

_____

_____

_____

_____

What Can You Learn from Them?

- *One thing I can try to emulate: (Write one habit, behavior, or trait they demonstrate that you'd like to adopt.)*

- *One way they inspire me to show up better in friendships: (Write one specific way they motivate you to improve your own approach to relationships.)*

_____

_____

_____

_____

Reflection Write a sentence or two about how this exercise has changed the way you think about or approach your friendships.

(Example: "This exercise helped me realize how much I value consistency in a friend, and I want to show the same reliability to the people I care about.")

_____

_____

_____

_____

Friendship Compatibility Checklist

Purpose: A checklist to assess compatibility in both existing and new friendships.

Instructions: Use this checklist as a guide to reflect on the health and fulfillment of your current friendships or when considering new ones.

Checklist

Questions	Yes	No
Boundaries: Do we respect each other's boundaries?		
Communication: Are our communication styles compatible or adaptable?		
Values: Do we share core values or interests?		
Reliability: Does this person follow through on commitments? Do I?		
Flexibility: Are they open to learning about and accommodating my needs? Am I open to theirs?		
Energy Balance: Does being with them feel energizing rather than draining for both of us?		
Support: Can I rely on them during challenging times? Can they rely on me?		
Growth: Do I feel like this friendship encourages personal growth for both of us?		
Trust: Is there a foundation of honesty and mutual respect?		

How to Use the Friendship Compatibility Checklist

Interpreting the Results

- **Mostly "Yes" Responses:** Indicates a strong foundation for compatibility and growth. These friendships are worth nurturing.

- **Mixed Responses:** Suggest areas to explore further. Discuss potential improvements or set boundaries where needed.

- **Mostly "No" Responses:** May signal a mismatch in core values or needs. Consider whether this friendship serves your well-being.

Reflecting on Your Friendships

Periodically review the checklist to assess your friendships. Identify strengths to celebrate and areas where there's room for improvement. Use these insights to:

- Nurture healthy relationships.

- Address potential challenges.

- Recognize when a friendship may no longer serve your well-being. Go slow in the case of long-term relationships. Remember, you can't make new old friends.

Friendship Action Plan

Purpose: A step-by-step guide to actively strengthen and nurture friendships.

Instructions: Use the steps below to take deliberate actions in your relationships.

Create Your 6-Step Action Plan

Step 1: Choose a Friendship to Nurture

• Identify one green-flag friendship you want to invest in.

_____

_____

_____

_____

Step 2: Plan an Action

• Think of a meaningful way to show appreciation, such as writing a heartfelt note, scheduling a call, or offering a small gesture like bringing them their favorite treat.

_____

_____

_____

_____

Step 3: Reflect on Your Own Role

- Consider one personal behavior you can improve for your friends (e.g., better communication, showing up more consistently, or respecting their boundaries more intentionally).

_____

_____

_____

_____

Step 4: Set a Goal

- Write down one specific goal for this friendship (e.g., spend more time together, have a deeper conversation, or plan an activity you'll both enjoy).

_____

_____

_____

_____

Step 5: Follow Through

- Schedule a time to take action and reflect on how it was received.

_____

_____

_____

_____

Step 6: Evaluate and Adjust

• After completing the plan, consider what worked well and what you might do differently in the future to strengthen the friendship further.

_____

_____

_____

_____

Decoding Involuntary Sounds

I make involuntary sounds... all the time. They can catch people off guard as much as they do me. They're usually attributed to my "quirkiness," but really, they're tied to differences in my sensory processing, emotional regulation, and motor control.

Sounds Are Responses to Triggers

These involuntary sounds don't happen in isolation—they're responses to my body's internal or external triggers. Sometimes they help me regulate when I'm feeling overwhelmed, and other times they're expressions of joy or surprise that bypass conscious thought. Here are three examples of how these responses can vary for me based on the situation:

- **Unconscious Vocal Stimming**

I was a passenger in a car when the driver approached a cloverleaf ramp to merge onto the highway. She hit the accelerator hard to join traffic, and the car surged forward in a way that caught me off guard. Without thinking, I let out a loud "wooooo." I didn't even realize I'd made the sound until she turned to me with a curious expression.

I've learned that this is **vocal stimming**, a self-regulating behavior triggered by the sudden motion and the unease it caused. The involuntary sound was my body's way of self-soothing and stabilizing.

- **Autonomic Response**

I was at a classical concert (while wearing earplugs), and at the end of the first piece, I clapped. My husband turned to me and said, "Wow, you must have really liked that work." Confused, I asked why he thought that, and he said, "You whooped out loud." I insisted I hadn't, and we moved on. Then, after the second piece, I clapped again, and he made the same comment. Finally, at the end of the third piece, we looked at each other, and as I started to protest that I wasn't whooping, I caught myself mid-sound—I had been whooping without realizing it.

This was an **autonomic response**, which is an involuntary action my body used to express joy and excitement. The reaction bypassed the conscious filter many people have, allowing me to express myself directly.

- **Hyper-Connected Sensory Processing**

When I talk about wind, I often don't just describe it; I'll make a whooshing noise that mimics the sound of it blowing through trees. If I'm talking about driving, I might also imitate the sound of a car engine revving. If I'm talking about a siren, I might also imitate its wail.

These are examples of **hyper-connected sensory processing**. My brain doesn't separate words from the sensory experiences they represent. Instead, it weaves them all together. In this case, the word "wind" isn't just a concept—it's tied to the actual experience of wind, including how it sounds, feels, smells, or even looks.

These are just some of the reasons why someone might make involuntary sounds, but there are many others. If you'd like to explore further, I encourage you to talk to a therapist or look for additional resources on the subject.

What can be confusing is that sometimes I make these sounds and some-times I don't. I believe it goes back to my sensory diet (am I overwhelmed?), how emotionally engaged I am with the topic (am I particularly excited?), the social context (am I masking?), and my cognitive load (am I having to think so hard in a conversation that I don't have the energy to make sounds?).

I admit that earlier in my life I saw my involuntary sounds as a deficit. Now, as I've gotten older and understand them and what's happening with my brain, it's quite the opposite. These sounds are an additional way to express what I'm thinking and feeling, almost like speaking another language. At times, the sounds may surprise others, but they're an honest reflection of why and how I communicate.

The Essentials:

Deciding When and How
to Share That You're Autistic

- Disclose your autism thoughtfully: for care, connection, or to support someone else.

- Remember that once your disclosure is out in the world, you can't take it back.

- Reactions will vary; most commonly, you'll encounter curiosity, support, or skepticism.

- Use three guiding questions before responding to disbelief: Do I care? Do I have the energy? What tone will I take?

- Canned responses save emotional energy and help address misunderstandings.

- Letting go of what doesn't support you clears the way for relationships that do.

Deciding When and How to Share That You're Autistic

Deciding whether or when to tell someone you're on the spectrum is a personal decision unique to you, your comfort level, and your circumstances. I don't have the magic answer for whether or how to do so, but I can share how I approach it.

I'm not ashamed of being autistic, but I don't want it to define me. It's part of who I am—just like my height, my brown hair, or my brown eyes. A piece of the whole, not the entire picture. I want people to see all of me, not just my diagnosis.

For that reason, I've been selective (until now) about sharing this part of myself.

I generally share that I'm autistic in four circumstances:

Disclosing my autism is situational: for care, connection, or when it can help others.

1. **When it's necessary for care, such as with medical professionals who need the information to deliver quality treatment (see the "Successfully Managing Medical Environments" chapter).**

Reactions have ranged from curious to entirely matter-of-fact, the latter especially with younger doctors, one of whom mentioned that autism is now a standard part of medical training, which is great news. All were supportive.

As part of receiving care, it's standard to check in online in advance and complete a medical history questionnaire. That process hasn't always run quite as smoothly.

I was surprised when the checklist for a major hospital grouped "autism" and "mental retardation" together under pre-existing conditions. I checked the box, and in that instance, a well-intentioned staff member called to help me navigate their medical portal, speaking slowly as if to a child, out of concern that I wouldn't be able to figure it out on my own.

For about a second, I was angry. Then, I burst out laughing and viewed the encounter as a teaching moment. I very politely thanked her for her concern (which seemed entirely genuine and friendly) and shared what I did for a living. I then only half-jokingly offered to rewrite the portal's user interface for free if they'd consider rethinking how they categorize patients on the spectrum.

I bring this up to show that while intentions may be good, sometimes the execution of those intentions is lacking. I do think that over time we'll learn more about autism, and the situation will improve. Until then, I give everyone a pass for at least caring enough to try and help.

2. When I've unintentionally wounded someone with my words or actions.

I was going through a dark time, barely managing to take care of myself. Then, the pandemic hit. At the same time, a vulnerable friend truly needed me, and I wasn't there for her. Worse, I "ghosted" her because I couldn't cope. She didn't know that I was autistic or what I was going through.

After the pandemic, when we could meet in person again, she asked to get together for coffee. She explained how much I had hurt her and asked why I cut our friendship off so abruptly. What had she done wrong?

I was devastated that I caused her such pain. In that moment, I shared that I was on the spectrum and talked about my struggles. She forgave me, although I know the hurt I caused forever damaged our friendship. I regret to this day that I waited too long to tell her. As a result, I'm now much more open to disclosing my diagnosis.

3. When I think sharing my diagnosis can help others.

At a dinner party, the woman seated next to me told me that her adult son was autistic and struggling. She was clearly anguished and couldn't comprehend what her son was going through. She wanted to be supportive but didn't know how.

I surprised myself by sharing my own diagnosis with a perfect stranger. Because my verbal skills are often strong, I was able to explain, in a way she could understand, what her son might be experiencing and suggest possible ways to help him. What works for me may not work for him, but it's a start.

This interaction is also part of why I'm writing this book and putting it out into the world. I'm normally a private person, and it's difficult to share something so personal. My hope is that the lessons I've learned can help others and that the benefit outweighs my discomfort.

4. **When I feel completely, 100% safe, and I want to share the truest part of myself with someone.**

My inner circle knows I'm on the spectrum. When I told each of them, with one exception, all were completely supportive. Their reactions ranged from "Things make so much more sense now," to "Thank you for trusting me enough to tell me," to curiosity about my experience and questions about how they could support me.

In some cases, it added a temporary awkwardness. I caught one friend surreptitiously watching me in social situations, observing my behavior. At first, it felt like I had become a zoo animal on display rather than just being myself. I could tell she was trying to reconcile my disclosure with how she had always seen me. While it was an uncomfortable phase, it eventually faded as she grew to understand me better.

In another instance, I was staying in the home of a friend who went out of her way to ensure my comfort. She asked if it was okay to vacuum because of the noise and checked whether keeping the TV on with the background movement would bother me. I was incredibly grateful for her thoughtfulness, but at the same time, I felt conflicted—I didn't want to create a burden for her as her guest. This, too, faded over time as we found a balance.

Reactions to My Disclosure

If I had to sum up the reactions to my disclosure, I'd say that most people who know me well weren't surprised when I shared my diagnosis. Up until that point, I was labeled quirky, with my love of math and science doing a lot of the explaining of my behavior for me.

I did frequently get one question, though: many asked why I chose to wait as long as I did to tell them.

The reasons are complicated. The shortest answer is that after disclosure, there's often an awkward phase, as I mentioned, where our relationship resets and finds its footing again. This intermediary period can be exhausting, as there are often a lot of questions for which I may not have answers. It forces me to dig deep, like in a therapy session. The good news is that the more people I tell, the more answers I find, and the more resilient I become.

As for the people who didn't know me well (like my dinner party companion), they often express disbelief. This reflects a lack of understanding about how autism can present differently in each person.

When Someone Questions Your Autism

How should you respond to people who don't believe you? I remind myself that their disbelief likely stems from a lack of understanding rather than ill intent.

I try framing my response with three key questions:

1. **Do I care?** Do I value this relationship enough to invest my time and energy into addressing their disbelief or misunderstandings? If the answer is yes, the next thing I ask myself is whether I have the energy to follow through.

2. **How full is my emotional bank account?** Do I have the capacity right now, or would it feel draining and unproductive? If I have the capacity, the next thing I decide on is the tone of my response.

Ask yourself three questions before responding to disbelief: Do I care? Do I have the energy? What tone do I want to take?

If the answer to either question is no, that's okay. Walk away, at least for now. You can always revisit the conversation later if you care but don't have the energy to engage in the moment.

3. I think about the tone I want to take, and I frame my options as warm, guarded, or nuclear.

   - **A warm response** means the encounter isn't emotionally charged. The person I'm educating genuinely wants to understand my autism. There's no judgment, and I feel safe having an honest, open conversation where I can be vulnerable.

   - **A guarded response** is somewhere between the vulnerability of warm and the scorched earth of nuclear. There's usually something holding me back. Maybe it's uncertainty about the other person's intentions or a need to protect myself. A guarded response balances patience with firmness, ensuring my needs are respected without escalating the situation.

- **A nuclear response** is reserved for situations where I feel disrespected, mocked, dismissed, or attacked. It's straight to the point, no sugarcoating, and makes it crystal clear where my boundaries are and how serious I am. While it's not my first choice, sometimes it's necessary when a person's actions or words require a firm correction.

This is a lot to think through in the middle of a conversation—too much. That's why I keep canned responses ready to go. It saves me from those moments afterward when I catch myself thinking, "I wish I had said that instead!"

Prepare canned responses for common misconceptions—it saves emotional energy and avoids second-guessing later.

The more people you tell, the more practice you'll get, and your response will become second nature.

How I might respond to: *"Well, you don't look autistic."*

Warm: *"That's a common misconception. Autism varies widely from person to person, and it's not always visible. It's about how my brain processes things."*

Guarded: *"I get where you're coming from, but autism isn't something you can tell by looking at someone. It's more about how we experience and interact with the world. That's why understanding autism as a spectrum is so important—it looks different for everyone."*

Nuclear: *"That's an offensive take. Autism isn't something you 'look' like; it's how my brain is wired, and dismissing it based on appearances is ignorant and harmful."*

I'm not being totally honest here with my nuclear response. This is a cleaned-up G-rated version of what I'd really say. I mean, I'm human.

A Necessary Goodbye

I mentioned that there was one exception to receiving support after sharing my diagnosis. In hindsight, maybe I couldn't have anticipated her exact words, but I could have anticipated her reaction based on the progression of our friendship. When I told her, she seemed to accept my diagnosis on the surface but was dismissive and wholly unsupportive.

Prior, there had been signs that our friendship was fracturing. I didn't want to give up on her or us, and it took a lot of soul-searching and many years on my part, but today we aren't friends. I don't believe it's because I told her that I'm on the spectrum. Rather, her reaction was the final red flag that made me realize our friendship wasn't a healthy one for me (in fairness, it may not have been for her, either). Letting go was difficult, but it gave me the space to focus instead on other relationships that are mutually supportive and nurturing.

Walking away from a relationship that doesn't support you makes room for ones that do.

Sharing with Intention

At some point, if you haven't already, you'll have to decide whether, when, and how to tell people. While I've decided to be open publicly by writing this book, I encourage you to be deliberate about your own approach. Once you share that you're autistic, especially in a world dominated by digital communication and social media, it's not something you can easily take back.

That said, sharing this part of yourself can be freeing and open the door to deeper, more authentic connections. When you're ready, you might find that the people who really matter will embrace you for exactly who you are. And if they don't, find people who will. We're out there.

⁙ **Tool:** Personalized Script Builder

Conversations about autism can be unpredictable. Preparing responses ahead of time can help you handle them with confidence. This tool helps you craft responses in different tones—warm, guarded, or firm—so you can decide how to engage in the moment without second-guessing later.

Step 1: Reflect on the Intent

Before crafting your response, consider the intent behind the statement:

- Is the person genuinely misinformed and open to learning?
- Are they being dismissive or disrespectful?
- Do you have the energy to engage?

Step 2: Choose Your Tone

Your tone might shift depending on your energy, the relationship, or how often you've had to address similar comments. Remember, you're in control. If you don't feel comfortable responding, it's okay to disengage or revisit later.

- **Warm:** For well-meaning but misinformed comments.
- **Guarded:** For unclear intentions or when setting a boundary is important.
- **Nuclear:** For dismissive or harmful comments requiring firm correction.

Step 3: Fill in Your Script

Using the guidance below, jot down your own responses to practice delivering them in a way that feels natural to you. You don't have to fill them all in—focus on the ones that feel most helpful and skip any that don't speak to you.

- **Warm:** *Acknowledge their comment and offer an educational explanation.*
- **Guarded:** *Set a boundary while correcting the misunderstanding.*
- **Nuclear:** *Nuclear responses are direct and unapologetic. Use this tone if you feel strongly about setting a firm boundary or addressing disrespect head-on. Feel free to skip this tone if it's not you.*

This script builder is a tool you can return to, refining responses as you encounter different situations. The goal isn't to memorize perfect responses to every scenario. It's to give you practice so you feel prepared, not pressured, when the moment arises.

Response: *"Well, you don't look autistic."*
Explanation: A common misconception about how autism presents.

Warm Tone:	
Guarded Tone:	
Nuclear Tone:	

Response: *"But you don't seem autistic at all. You're so social!"*
Explanation: Focusing on social skills.

Warm Tone:	
Guarded Tone:	
Nuclear Tone:	

Response: *"You're just quirky. I wouldn't call that autism."*
Explanation: A dismissive statement questioning the diagnosis itself.

Warm Tone:

Guarded Tone:

Nuclear Tone:

Response: *"Everyone's a little on the spectrum these days."*
Explanation: A broad, invalidating comment about the legitimacy of autism.

Warm Tone:

Guarded Tone:

Nuclear Tone:

Response: *"Oh, so what kind of special talents do you have? Like Rain Man?"*
Explanation: Informed by media-driven stereotypes.

Warm Tone:	
Guarded Tone:	
Nuclear Tone:	

Response: *"You must be really mild. I know someone with autism, and they can't even talk."*
Explanation: A comparative comment about severity, reinforcing stereotypes.

Warm Tone:	
Guarded Tone:	
Nuclear Tone:	

Response: *"Are you sure it's not just a phase or overdiagnosis?"*
Explanation: Challenging the legitimacy of the diagnosis.

Warm Tone:	
Guarded Tone:	
Nuclear Tone:	

Response: *"You must have outgrown it, though—you seem fine now."*
Explanation: A misconception about autism changing or disappearing over time.

Warm Tone:	
Guarded Tone:	
Nuclear Tone:	

Response: *"I thought autism only affected kids. How did you get diagnosed as an adult?"*

Explanation: A misunderstanding about adult diagnosis.

Warm Tone:	
Guarded Tone:	
Nuclear Tone:	

Response: *"I've never seen you have a meltdown, so I wouldn't have guessed."*

Explanation: Focusing on behaviors, implying misunderstanding of the spectrum.

Warm Tone:	
Guarded Tone:	
Nuclear Tone:	

The Essentials:

Setting Yourself Up for Success at Social Gatherings

- Assess events in advance to identify stressors and plan strategies that fit your needs.

- Use a self-assessment matrix to clarify your comfort levels for transportation, event types, and participation.

- Decide your limits ahead of time and honor them—it's okay to decline or leave early.

- Small preparations, like eating beforehand or planning your outfit, can make a big difference.

- Have an exit strategy ready to leave quietly and on your own terms.

- Social success isn't about perfection—it's about finding ways to participate safely and comfortably.

Setting Yourself Up for Success at Social Gatherings

I pulled a bright pink envelope from the mailbox. The sender had taken the time to write my address in gold, metallic ink, and it had a creative custom stamp. Inside was an invitation to a friend's party printed on a background she had hand-painted. It was a hosted brunch where she was gathering some of her favorite people in her home to celebrate an upcoming birthday. I liked the host a great deal, and anyone who took this much care with the invitation would likely throw a lovely party. I was excited, my calendar was free, and I dashed off my affirmative RSVP.

And then I immediately regretted it.

I like the idea of attending social gatherings. The reality? Not always.

Like many others, I crave connection—especially after the isolation of the pandemic. In the moment, I imagine the best-case scenario: meeting interesting people, having great conversations, and enjoying myself.

I also genuinely love seeing other people enjoying themselves, laughing, and coming together.

Perhaps there's a bit of optimism too. Somehow, I convince myself this time will be different. But as the event approaches, I start to worry about the potential for overstimulation, the small talk, the missed social cues, and the inevitable exhaustion that comes after.

I'm drained before I even leave my house.

That's when I realized that to be able to spend time with the people I care about without undue stress, I needed to set myself up for success. I needed to pace myself—it's a marathon and not a sprint—and find ways to conserve my energy (see the chapter "Masking, Unmasking, and Finding Balance" for more information).

Plan ahead, pace yourself, and protect your energy— social success starts there.

I started thinking through the elements of gatherings that were stressful, and considered the elements that were less so. Then, I came up with strategies to address them.

Much of this process was self-discovery. I knew what my major triggers were, but I was less aware of the smaller, more nuanced triggers that cumulatively added up to a big impact on me.

Managing these required a deeper level of self-awareness and a more deliberate approach.

Understanding Event Impact

To figure this out, I did a self-assessment to better understand my comfort levels with:

- Different transportation methods
- Various event types
- How long I can comfortably stay
- The types of participation I enjoy
- Activities that feel energizing vs. draining

This approach has been a huge help in planning and preparing for events in ways that minimize stress and maximize enjoyment.

Here's a sample self-assessment, where the categories are generic, but the assessment is mine. Feel free to customize it and try for yourself to see if it can help. If a matrix feels too formal, use it as a guideline and ask yourself the questions mentally, or adapt it in a way that better fits your needs.

Transportation To/From Event:

Preference	Very Comfortable	Somewhat Comfortable	Neutral	Somewhat Uncomfortable	Very Uncomfortable
Arrive alone	X				
Ride with others					X
Use public transit		X			
Use a ride hail or taxi				X	
Drive, walk, or bike	X				
Get dropped off				X	

I prefer to drive, walk, or bike to an event—and to arrive alone. Riding with others is harder. The social dynamics can feel unpredictable, and I may not be able to leave if I need to.

Taxis are stressful, but they're manageable. It's just one interaction, not many.

Public transit is the wild card. I never know what I'm going to get, which can be unsettling, but I often find comfort in the ability to blend into the crowd and keep to myself.

Event Types:

Events	Very Comfortable	Somewhat Comfortable	Neutral	Somewhat Uncomfortable	Very Uncomfortable
Large parties				X	
Small parties		X			
Family events					X
Friends' gatherings		X			
Celebrations (weddings, birthdays, etc.)				X	
Community and school events				X	
Structured agendas	X				
Unstructured socializing					X
Events with alcohol	X				
Events with pets	X				
Events with children		X			
Loud events					X
Quiet events	X				

I'm most comfortable at quiet, low-key events—especially when there's structure or familiar faces.

Large, loud gatherings are harder. If socializing is unstructured or I don't know many people, the challenge increases.

Events with pets or children tend to be easier to navigate. They add natural points of engagement and give me something to focus on.

Familiar faces, quiet spaces, and structured activities make events more manageable.

Event Duration:

Preference	Very Comfortable	Somewhat Comfortable	Neutral	Somewhat Uncomfortable	Very Uncomfortable
Less than 1 hour		X			
1 – 2 hours				X	
2 – 3 hours					X
3 – 4 hours					X
4+ hours					X

I'm most comfortable with shorter events—an hour or less is ideal.

Longer events take more energy. Managing them requires extra tools, and recovery time afterward increases.

I factor this into my decision. Will attending drain me so much that I miss out on something more important later?

Forms of Participation:

Preference	Very Comfortable	Somewhat Comfortable	Neutral	Somewhat Uncomfortable	Very Uncomfortable
One-on-one				X	
Small groups		X			
Large groups			X		
Public speaking			X		
Leading discussions	X				
Listening only	X				
Contributing as a participant				X	

I'm most comfortable in listening roles or leading discussions. Leading lets me prepare in advance and shape the outcome.

One-on-one interactions feel unpredictable, which makes them harder.

Large groups and public speaking depend on the situation. I like blending into a crowd, but if it's loud, it can be overwhelming. Public speaking is fine if I know the topic well—less so if I don't.

Activities:

Preference	Very Comfortable	Somewhat Comfortable	Neutral	Somewhat Uncomfortable	Very Uncomfortable
Dancing	X				
Playing games			X		
Watching performances	X				
Singing or karaoke				X	
Eating or dining together				X	
Participating in sports		X			

I feel comfortable dancing and playing sports, which surprises me—I'm not the most graceful person. But movement is soothing, which makes both activities easier.

Watching performances is another safe zone. They keep my brain engaged, and with earplugs, I can prevent overstimulation.

Put it all together, and my ideal event is:

- Small, structured, and quiet
- Arriving alone
- Familiar faces, pets, or children
- One hour or less
- Opportunities to listen or lead discussions

Dancing, sports, and performances? Enjoyable—as long as I can manage the sensory load.

Sign me up!

When to Say Yes or No

I don't want my RSVP to events to automatically be a no, which was my inclination before the self-assessment. However, I also don't want it to be an automatic yes just because I fear that I'm isolating myself, and then suffer the consequences of too much stimulation after the fact. The matrix serves as a level set for how a gathering might impact me, and from there, I can make a more informed decision about attending.

Using my matrix as a guide, if I get invited to an event where I can arrive alone, it has structured activities, it might include wine and pets, is quiet, and I can stay for less than an hour, there's a good chance I can make it through the event successfully.

On the other hand, if I get invited to a small event that will last for several hours of loud, unstructured socializing, and where I'll have to arrive with a group, history has taught me (and my matrix suggests) that there's a good chance I'll struggle.

In that case, I might decline the event, or I might still attend because it's important to someone I care about. If I do go, after completing the matrix, I'm better equipped to understand the potential stress load, and I can take precautions to protect myself.

Know your limits, set boundaries,
and give yourself permission to leave early.

Before I Head Out

I've decided to attend—even if it might be difficult. But I can set myself up for success. Here's how:

- **Gather additional information about the event.** Without burdening the host with too many questions, I try to find out as much as I can about the event that wasn't already in the invitation. I might look up the venue online for photos and reviews, or ask mutual friends who I know will also be attending.

- **Make sure I've eaten... something.** Even if I'm attending a dinner party, I don't want to arrive famished and with the resulting low energy levels that may make the party more difficult for me. I will eat a small meal beforehand and keep a bag of nuts in my bag to ensure that a lack of food won't hurt my chances of having an enjoyable time.

- **Dress comfortably.** I wear clothes that make me feel confident and comfortable, and I avoid anything that might cause sensory discomfort. Special events often require clothes other than what I wear every day. In those cases, I do a trial run of the outfit. I may first wear it to a low-stakes gathering, or I may simply wear it around the house for an afternoon.

- **Plan transportation.** If I'm taking a taxi or a ride hail, I'll sit directly behind the driver to minimize conversation. If I'm on public transit, I'll wear earplugs (while remaining aware of my surroundings for safety reasons). If I have no choice but to ride with others to the event, I will try to at least leave on my own and when I'm ready.

- **Set limits in advance.** I decide beforehand how long I'll stay, although if things are going well, I give myself the flexibility to remain longer. Since things can get chaotic once I'm at a party, I set a check-in alarm on my phone before I leave the house.

- **Prepare a few conversation starters.** Beyond the usual small talk like, "How are you?" or "What are your plans for (insert upcoming holiday)?" or "How was your (insert recent holiday)?", I think of a few topics that others might find interesting and that I also find interesting. One friend told me that when she's speaking with couples, she always asks how they met because many people enjoy sharing that story. Taking her advice, I've found that it works well for me too.

- **Have an exit strategy.** At some point, I'll need to leave, likely far earlier than the rest of the guests. I want to exit quietly and graciously without interrupting the flow of the party. I'll wait for a natural break in the party, such as after a toast, and will discreetly say to the host something along the lines of, "Thank you so much for inviting me; I had a great time. I need to head out now, but I hope the rest of the event is wonderful." And then I quickly exit without causing a disruption or drawing too much attention to myself.

- **Limit activities before and after the event.** Considering my sensory diet plan (see the chapter "How to Build a Sensory Diet That Keeps You Balanced"), I make sure I have downtime and calming activities planned to help recharge and decompress.

At the Event

I have several tactics to use once I'm at the event. I don't use them all—sometimes I may only use one or two—but it's comforting to know I have options.

I mix and match these tactics based on the situation and how I'm feeling. I find these approaches particularly helpful:

- **Time your arrival and departure.** I arrive early to the event before it gets too crowded, but not so early that I'm the first person there. I leave once the party gets loud and is in full swing. I call this the "Goldilocks" moment—when the party isn't too busy or too empty, but just right. I implement my previously planned exit strategy and make a quiet departure without disrupting the event.

Small tweaks make a big difference. Arrive at the right time. Bring a snack. Protect your energy.

- **Find quiet spaces to recharge.** I scout restrooms, bedrooms (while respecting the host's privacy), outdoor areas, balconies, and out-of-the-way corners as potential places of respite should I need them. I might have to "take a phone call" or "check on something for work." I avoid calling attention to myself by not staying in one place for too long or stepping away from the party too frequently. Otherwise, well-intentioned people may become concerned about me, and then I'll have to explain myself, which can be more stressful than if I skipped the break instead.

- **Engage with family pets and children.** Petting animals is soothing for me. If there are kids, I might sit on the floor and play with them. They don't seem to mind silence, or I can ask them questions, which often yield interesting answers.

- **Volunteer to assist the host.** Having something to focus on is relaxing, plus I like helping. It gives me a sense of purpose and allows me to engage in the event at my own pace. Tasks like refilling drinks, arranging food, or cleaning up can provide a welcome distraction from small talk and give me a reason to move around without feeling awkward. Additionally, it offers an opportunity to interact with guests in a more structured and comfortable way.

- **Make "laps" around the party.** I find the movement of walking soothing, and by walking around and occasionally stopping, I can engage in ways I'm comfortable while at the same time actively engaging in the party.

- **Use the pre-thought-out conversation topics.** Listen, observe, and follow your conversation partner's lead. Pay attention to any visible clues about a person's interests. If someone is wearing a shirt with a band logo, I might ask about their favorite music. If someone mentions enjoying movies, I might bring up a recent film I've seen. If they talk about their pets, I might share a related story about animals. Then, if needed, I always have my pre-thought-out conversation topics to deploy. If a conversation becomes too overwhelming, it's okay to excuse yourself politely. I might say, "I'm going to refresh my drink," or "I promised to help in the kitchen. It was nice talking to you," and then move on, continuing my laps around the party.

- **Have your photograph taken.** I strongly dislike having my photo taken, so it may seem counterintuitive when I say that I try to be included in gathering photos if there are any. I do this for two reasons: First, as it reminds the host of my attendance, especially if I've had to take breaks from the group to recharge. And second, when I later view the photos, they motivate me to attend future gatherings, to put myself out there, since photos often depict happy times.

- **Know when it's time to leave.** Even if my check-in alarm hasn't reached its limit, there may be signs that I should leave, such as needing time in quiet spaces more frequently, needing to stay in the quiet spaces longer, or if I feel a down coming on. In that case, I execute my pre-planned exit strategy and leave.

Recharge

Following my pre-planning, I limit my social interactions after the event to recharge. I might refer to my sensory diet plan to see how to get back on track. I might sleep more, listen to relaxing music, or hike.

Sometimes, I get lucky, or perhaps my planning and tactics were particularly effective, and my anticipated low energy levels don't materialize. Regardless, I reflect on the event, noting what worked and what didn't. This helps me make course corrections for future gatherings.

Reflecting on events is important so that you don't have to start from scratch each time. Once you've attended enough of them and know what does and doesn't work for you, you can reuse the strategies and tactics again and again, making minor course corrections as needed. With a bit of effort in the beginning, you'll find that social gatherings become much more manageable and maybe even enjoyable.

As soon as I'm able, I send a thank you to the host, whether by text, phone call, or written note—whatever is right for the occasion. This has nothing to do with being on the spectrum but is my way of respecting the host and appreciating that they went out of their way to show me kindness by including me in their event.

Ready for the Next Step?

Hosting events like themed dinner parties, group yoga sessions for friends, nights out at the theater, dance classes, art crawls, literary salons, and taco crawls might not seem like something I'd enjoy—but I do. Successfully attending social events over time gave me the courage to take the next step. Why attend someone else's event where I have to manage my anxiety and sensory sensitivities when, instead, by making the effort, I can craft a get-together that suits my needs while also providing a fun event for my friends?

Using my gathering matrix as a guide, I can set the activity, the food, the guests, the duration, and the environment—with the goal of it being an enjoyable experience for everyone, not just me. And as the host, I automatically stay busy with event details, giving me activities that help me remain focused and feeling less awkward.

Ultimately, I'm not naturally wired to attend or host events. It's a deliberate choice to engage, and if I'm going to do so, I want it to be a positive experience.

Equipped for Success

I normally think through my comfort matrix deliberately when RSVPing to an event, but something unusual happened recently.

I received an invitation that I didn't hesitate to accept without looking at my matrix, and that feeling carried through the event and until I arrived back home after. I had no anxiety, I had a great time, and I didn't have to recover much afterward.

The event was a one-hour presentation on an art movement I wanted to learn more about, followed by a brief cocktail reception. I could even take the subway.

It checked all the right boxes—short, predictable, and intellectually engaging, with just enough socializing tied to the topic.

I've built up a kind of muscle memory for events that suit me, allowing me to trust my instincts without always needing to reference my matrix. It's not that I was incapable of socializing all these years; I just hadn't yet found the right tools.

It's not about avoiding events—
it's about being equipped to participate
in ways that feel safe and manageable.

In the end, for me, it's not about avoiding events or hiding from sensory or social situations—it's about being equipped to participate in ways that feel safe and manageable.

With the right strategies, I can not only attend more events, I can truly participate and enjoy them.

And that's the real win.

⠸ Tool: Pre-Event Prep Checklist

After filling in your self-assessment, you've decided to attend an event. Now what? This checklist is designed to help you prepare for social gatherings with confidence and ease. Each section outlines specific tasks to complete before the event. Feel free to adapt it to fit your needs and priorities.

Research the Event

o   Refer back to the "Setting Yourself Up for Success at Social Gatherings" chapter for tips.
o   Look up the venue online (photos, reviews, layout).
o   Check the event schedule (structured vs. unstructured activities).
o   Ask mutual friends who are attending about the crowd or setting.

Plan Your Outfit

o   Select clothes that feel comfortable and make you feel confident.
o   Do a trial run of your outfit if it's something you don't usually wear.
o   Consider bringing earplugs or noise-canceling headphones for noisy environments.

Prepare for Conversations

o   Think of a few conversation starters (e.g., "What's the most exciting thing you've done this week?" or "How do you know [the host]?").
o   Reflect on safe topics of interest to you and others (movies, hobbies, pets).

Eat Beforehand

o   Have a small meal to avoid feeling hungry or low-energy.
o   Keep a light snack in your bag for later, if needed.

Review Your Limits

o   Decide how long you'll stay. Remember that you can always stay longer if you're comfortable.
o   Set a timer or reminder on your phone to check in with yourself during the event.

Plan Transportation

o   Confirm how you'll get there and back to minimize stimulation (public transport, ride-share, driving).

o   If you're relying on others, arrange backup options for leaving when you're ready.

With everything in place, you're ready to have a great time.

Enjoy your event!

Autism vs. Introversion: What's the Difference?

When sharing my party prep with a friend who describes himself as an introvert, he pointed out the commonalities between us. As an introvert, he too struggles with social exhaustion, difficulty making small talk, feeling overwhelmed in large groups, and the need for downtime after events. He asked, in a gentle and curious way, what was so different between us.

I enjoy thoughtful, well-meaning questions like this. He was making an effort to understand our similarities and differences, which, in turn, strengthened our friendship.

While I can't speak to an introvert's point of view, here's what I believe the differences are:

- **Nature:** Introversion is a personality trait—it affects how someone recharges and how much solitude they need. Autism isn't just about personality; it's a difference in how I process the world. While both shape social experiences, autism influences far more than just my energy levels.

- **Social Interaction:** Introverts may find social situations draining, but they can usually manage them without too much trouble. For me, there's the additional strain of decoding social cues, unwritten rules, and figuring out how to connect in ways that don't always come naturally.

- **Sensory Sensitivities:** Some introverts might not love bright lights or loud spaces, but for me, sensory sensitivity isn't just a preference—it's a built-in part of who I am. Sounds, textures, and even certain smells can be physically painful. And it's not just about social events—it's everywhere, all the time.

- **Managing Social & Sensory Load:** Introverts need downtime after socializing. I need more than that—I have to plan ahead for both social and sensory overload, adjusting my environment and sometimes avoiding situations entirely to stay balanced.

I'm not minimizing the very real issues experienced by introverts, merely pointing out our differences. Introversion is about energy management in social contexts, while for me autism involves broader differences in social communication, sensory processing, and behavior.

Interestingly, when I was younger and before I was diagnosed on the spectrum, I mistakenly thought I was an introvert, albeit an extreme one.

That belief led me to push through social struggles, thinking they were something to fix. When I couldn't meet those expectations, I felt inadequate.

Discovering that I was autistic reframed those challenges; it wasn't about trying harder to fit in, but about understanding my needs and creating strategies that worked for me.

The Essentials:

Big Life Events When You're the Center of Attention

- Define your non-negotiables early—they set boundaries for what matters most to you.

- Approach planning as a team effort—engage friends and family in ways that suit their strengths.

- Build an emotional support system into your event—identify people who can help you stay calm and on track.

- Anticipate potential challenges, like social dynamics or overstimulation, and plan ahead to address them.

- You can celebrate in a way that feels true to you—while also honoring the needs of those around you.

Big Life Events: When You're the Center of Attention

When I got married, my husband wanted a large wedding ceremony, and I very much didn't.

So we compromised.

I agreed that he could have the wedding he wanted on one condition: that all I had to do was show up and say the words "I do." I was a Bridezilla, but a different kind of Bridezilla—one who refused to engage.

On the other hand, my romantic husband was beyond excited to have a big party. The fancier, the better. He wanted flowers, a cake, a multi-course dinner, a live band for dancing, lots of photographs, and to hold the event in a high-profile venue. He wanted all of our friends, family, and people from long ago in his past, some of whom I hadn't met, to witness us say our vows and party the night away.

My husband thought I would come around and embrace wedding activities, but I was having none of it. I knew I had to protect myself.

Any time he asked me to do something related to the wedding, I reminded him of our deal: I only had to show up and say two words. He even joked to the wedding planner that she would get a bonus if I made it to the ceremony.

In the end, I honored my commitment, and he honored his. To this day my husband says our wedding was the best day of his life. Despite my limited involvement, the day was one of the most stressful I can remember, but I was happy to be able to do something that made my husband happy, while he still respected my needs.

That was my wedding experience. But milestone events in general don't come with just one challenge—they can come with many.

The Pressure of Being the Guest of Honor

Big life events are social gatherings on a much larger scale—weddings, birthdays, graduations, baby showers, and retirement parties. While each is different, they all share one challenge: When the celebration is about you, there's heightened expectation, social pressure, and the challenge of being the center of attention—whether you want it or not.

For autistic individuals, these added layers of social and logistical demands can be especially difficult. Even if we want to participate, we may still struggle to do so.

In the "Setting Yourself Up for Success at Social Gatherings" chapter, I covered tips on what to do if you're a guest at an event. But when the event is all about you, you can't exactly retreat to your quiet space in the middle of saying your vows. Special events require special planning.

Determine Your Non-Negotiables

I had only one goal for the wedding: to get through the celebration without a down. To do so, I firmly established boundaries, which I labeled as non-negotiables.

As I mentioned earlier, my non-negotiable was simply that I would show up to the ceremony and say two words without further engagement. Though it may seem flippant, it provided a clear way to communicate my limits.

If I had been feeling overwhelmed, I could refer to it and say no to activities without feeling guilty. It also served as a type of insurance policy. I knew that I had an exit strategy if needed, and that my husband would understand. It gave me courage and a safety net to put myself out there in ways I might not have otherwise.

But the wedding wasn't just about me. My husband's non-negotiables were that we wed in a specific venue that was meaningful to him and that the ceremony be in the evening.

Agreeing to our non-negotiables ahead of time set us up to understand where we could compromise—and where we couldn't. We were crystal clear on what was important to us individually and as a couple. Even then, we recognized that, for my sake, we needed to approach our wedding differently from a more traditional one.

This approach doesn't just apply to weddings. For a milestone birthday, your non-negotiable might be limiting the event to a small, intimate group rather than a large party. For a retirement celebration, you might decide that there will be no speeches, or that you'll attend the event but skip the post-party. Or perhaps in-person events won't work for you, and instead, you prefer virtual celebrations. Establishing these non-negotiables can be your lifeline for maintaining control during any big event.

Non-negotiables aren't selfish—they're the foundation for celebrating in a way that honors both your needs and those of the people around you.

"Outsource" Tasks and Engage Loved Ones

In many weddings, it's not uncommon for one partner to shoulder the bulk of the planning logistics due to desire, skills, or timing, while the other partner may chime in with support and opinions. In this way, our wedding was no different, as I had to severely limit any human interaction in the lead-up to the ceremony to give myself the best chance of getting through the day. And while my husband is a good planner and was looking forward to managing the details, it was still a lot for him to handle on his own.

That, combined with the fact that my husband is very social, made it especially challenging. Where's the fun in planning if he had to do all the work by himself?

We decided to "outsource" aspects of the wedding to our family and friends, and where we could, we turned the logistics into fun mini-events.

- The idea of reciting deeply personal wedding vows, even in front of people I loved, physically pained me, but at the same time, I recognized that vows were an important part of the wedding ritual. My husband, being the problem-solver that he is, came up with the concept of the *Content Collective*. Led by his sister and joined by a group of close friends, they mined details from their relationships with us and wrote what became our vow "script." Then, during the ceremony, each of our best friends recited the vows, as an officiant might, and all we had to do was say "I do." Unusual? Maybe, but it worked beautifully.

- A family member is an excellent cook and loves entertaining. When it came time for my husband to decide on the wedding menu, he reached out and asked her opinion. Her input was invaluable, and she did a great job.

- My husband took a friend who is a gifted baker with him to taste-test wedding cakes, but first they had lunch and made a day of it.

- Another friend is a magician with flowers, and she and my husband toured the Flower Market together, discussing ideas for the decor.

- When it came time to choose beverages for the wedding, my husband hosted a tasting for several of our friends. Another task was checked off the list.

The key is to make it easy (and ideally, fun) for people to participate in ways that are natural for them while consistent with what you desire and need for the event.

Design Support into the Event

I knew I couldn't get through the event without support, and I didn't shy away from asking for help. We built a support system into the process and planned for it just like anything else.

- **If possible, hire an event planner.** A full event planner is the most hands-on support but can be the priciest option. However, there are other options, such as hiring someone just for the day of the event or hiring a virtual assistant to make phone calls and interact with people in the lead-up to the event. The virtual assistant option can be particularly low-stress for those who may struggle with human interaction, because those interactions can be handled via email and text rather than in person or by phone. And this doesn't just apply to weddings—any large milestone event can benefit from hiring a planner.

- **Have a friend or family member serve as your go-to person for questions or issues that arise during the event.** This can leave you to focus on being present without the added stress of problem-solving.

Support doesn't happen by accident—build it into your event, just like any other detail.

- **If a seated dinner is involved, seat people you're most comfortable with near you.** This can really help ease any social pressure and keep anxiety at bay.

- **Identify a few of "your people" to check in on you throughout the event.** In my case, I established a signal that meant, "Please get me out of here!" This provided an easy way to be extracted from a stressful social encounter without having to navigate the social norms of asking directly. I wasn't the one trying to leave. Instead, my friends were pulling me away.

- **Task someone with reminding you to eat.** I'm not always in tune with what's going on with my body, and even on a regular day I can forget to eat. If my blood sugar drops, it can cause problems. To remedy this, have someone check in with you throughout the event and make sure you're eating something substantial. I learned the hard way at my wedding when I survived on nothing but sugar and wine—not a diet I recommend.

With a team behind me, I felt bolstered and ready for the celebration. Now, all I had to do was get through the day.

Staying Calm and Centered During the Celebration

With a few more adjustments, it's possible to stay centered and enjoy the celebration, or at least enjoy parts of it. Here are some things that worked for me:

- **In the case of weddings, have your people walk you down the aisle, or walk down the aisle together with your partner.** I didn't want the tradition of being "given away" by my father, so I had my three-year-old niece and five-year-old nephew walk with me. An added benefit is that they were so cute that they took some of the attention off me. For other events, like a graduation, you could sit with a small group of trusted friends or family during the ceremony to help calm your nerves. If you're celebrating a milestone birthday or retirement, consider having a friend or relative give a toast on your behalf if public speaking feels too overwhelming.

- **Pre-arrange check-ins with your partner or other significant people.** At my wedding, I had a quiet, private space for sensory breaks, but I also wanted to spend time with my husband. Right after the ceremony, he joined me there for a glass of Champagne. We would mingle at the party and then retreat to my quiet room to check in with each other. Sometimes, my husband would head back out to enjoy the party while I stayed behind, and that was perfectly fine with both of us.

- **Have a short script prepared for greeting guests and well-wishers.** You can keep it simple with "Thank you so much for coming. It means a lot to us. I hope you have (or are having or had, depending on timing) a great time." For me, it was more important to thank each guest than it was to personalize the message. I had to prioritize.

You can be the center of attention
and still prioritize your comfort and needs.

- **Decide and communicate your photography strategy in advance.** We let the photographer know beforehand that I would only be available for a short period for formal photos and asked that they focus on candid shots instead, where I wouldn't have to pose. During the event, I knew exactly how long I had to pose, which was blessedly short. When we received our photos back and I told my husband that there were far too many pictures of me, he replied, "That's right, you're the bride!" We had a good laugh.

- **Minimize the potential for drama.** We had two warring guests who couldn't be near each other without verbally scratching the other's eyes out. Unbeknownst to each of them, we tasked two good-natured friends with keeping them physically separated and content. Should we have had to do this? No, guests should behave themselves, but for me, it was better to be proactive and ensure that we wouldn't have to step in to avoid them causing drama. This small act gave me peace of mind.

Congratulations—you made it! Now, after the event, you can refer to previous chapters for ways to replenish and get back on track.

Respecting Both Our Needs

Even though my wedding was stressful, I don't regret it one bit. I appreciate that it was a rite of passage, it made my husband happy, and it taught me valuable skills that I now use in other areas of my life.

My husband got the wedding he wanted, full of the people and experiences that mattered to him. I got the space and boundaries I needed to make it through. Neither of us had to sacrifice entirely—we found a way to balance our needs.

However, every year on our anniversary, when he asks me to renew our vows, my answer is a lighthearted *no*.

Celebrate Without Overload

While celebrating in a way that is comfortable to you is ideal, external pressures to conform can make setting boundaries challenging. Even small adjustments can help honor your needs.

I recognize that not everyone has the luxury of opting out of milestone events the way I did, but even if that's not an option, there are solid tactics to help you get through the day. While my examples are focused on my wedding, many of these suggestions can be applied to any major milestone event.

In the end, finding ways to celebrate on your own terms is about making these moments meaningful and even joyful without sacrificing your well-being.

.: **Tool:** Big Life Event Preparation Questionnaire

This questionnaire is here to guide you through preparing for your event in a way that feels manageable and true to who you are. Think of this as a tool to help you clarify what you need and how to make the event work for you. Even if this event doesn't go exactly as planned, it's an opportunity to learn and refine your approach for your next event.

Comfort and Boundaries

- What is essential for your physical and sensory comfort?

_____

_____

_____

_____

- What situations or interactions might overwhelm you, and how can you avoid or manage them?

_____

_____

_____

- What boundaries do you need to set to feel safe and supported during the event?

_____

_____

_____

_____

Event Goals and Priorities

- What is the primary purpose of this event for you? How about for other stakeholders?

_____

_____

_____

_____

- What outcomes or experiences are most important for you to achieve during this event?

_____

_____

_____

_____

- What does success look like for you at this event?

_____

_____

_____

_____

Logistical Preferences

- What is your ideal timeframe for the event (e.g., duration, time of day)?

_____

_____

_____

_____

- How do you prefer to handle transportation to and from the event?

_____

_____

_____

_____

- Are there any specific tasks or responsibilities you prefer not to handle, and can you delegate them to friends and family?

_____

_____

_____

_____

Social Considerations

- Who are the key people you want present at this event?

_____

_____

_____

_____

- What types of social interactions are you comfortable with (e.g., one-on-one, small groups)?

_____

_____

_____

_____

- Are there any individuals you'd prefer to avoid, and how can this be handled respectfully?

_____

_____

_____

_____

Sensory Needs

- What environmental factors (e.g., noise, lighting, temperature) are critical for your comfort?

_____

_____

_____

_____

- Do you need a designated quiet space or sensory break area? If so, what should it include?

_____

_____

_____

_____

- What personal items (e.g., earplugs, fidgets) will help you manage sensory sensitivities?

_____

_____

_____

_____

Emotional Support

- Who can provide emotional support before, during, or after the event?

_____

_____

_____

_____

- What kind of check-ins or reassurances will help you feel grounded and supported?

_____

_____

_____

_____

- Do you have a signal or system in place for when you need assistance or a break?

_____

_____

_____

_____

Decision-Making and Compromise

- What aspects of the event are non-negotiable for you, and why?

_____

_____

_____

_____

- Which areas are you open to compromising on, and what conditions would make compromise acceptable?

_____

_____

_____

_____

- What are the most significant differences between your preferences and those of others involved, and how can they be reconciled?

_____

_____

_____

_____

Exit Strategies

- What is your plan for leaving the event if you become overwhelmed or need a break?

_____

_____

_____

_____

- Who can help you implement your exit strategy if needed?

_____

_____

_____

_____

- How can you communicate your exit plan in advance to avoid misunderstandings?

_____

_____

_____

_____

Celebration on Your Terms

- How can this event reflect your personality and values while still meeting the expectations of others?

_____

_____

_____

_____

- What unique elements would make the event feel meaningful and personal to you?

_____

_____

_____

_____

- What steps can you take to ensure this event feels like a celebration of you, not just for you?

_____

_____

_____

_____

After-Event Reflection

- How will you know if the event was successful for you?
- What strategies or boundaries would you revisit or revise for the next big life event?
- How will you prioritize rest and recovery after the event?

The Essentials:

Redefining Connection Beyond Eye Contact

- Eye contact can feel overwhelming and invasive, similar to "intimacy overload."

- Context matters: factors like energy levels, familiarity, and environment can impact the experience of making eye contact.

- "People hangover" describes the exhaustion that can result from prolonged or intense eye contact.

- Engagement doesn't have to rely on eye contact; alternative methods include verbal affirmations, physical gestures, and direct communication.

- Strengthening other non-verbal skills can provide an edge in under-standing people and situations.

Redefining Connection Beyond Eye Contact

In 2010, the artist Marina Abramović presented *The Artist is Present* at NYC's Museum of Modern Art. Every day for three months she invited visitors to sit in the chair opposite her, one at a time, and silently engage by making eye contact. Abramović sat motionless and silent, and gazing into the eyes of each visitor who chose to sit with her. The performance was about presence, and how unspoken communication occurs through direct eye contact. All of this, and with strangers.

When I first learned about this piece, my reaction was visceral. It sounded like my own personal hell.

For me, eye contact isn't just about looking at someone—it's an intimate act that can feel overwhelming and invasive.

Eye contact can feel like intimacy overload— too much connection, too quickly.

Even imagining sitting across from the artist left me feeling suffocated. A pressure builds in my chest whenever I try to hold eye contact, as if someone is squeezing my heart, and it intensifies until I have to look away. Abramović's performance might have been a profound exploration of connection for some, but for me, it highlights the challenges I face with something as seemingly simple as meeting someone's gaze.

For many people, eye contact may feel as natural as breathing—they don't have to think about it. In contrast, I need to spend considerable energy deciding where—or whether—to look, and if I do make eye contact, for how long. The effort can leave me completely exhausted.

While not everyone on the spectrum struggles with eye contact, for many of us, it's a common thread.

Eye Contact Challenges

The challenges of making eye contact can vary widely. Some people experience it as an invasion of personal space, while others feel overwhelmed by too much visual input. For some, it creates uncertainty about where to look or makes processing social cues more difficult. Others find it impossible to focus on conversation if they're also managing eye contact.

And then sometimes, making eye contact that would otherwise feel challenging is just fine. Context is everything. For me, other factors come into play, such as:

• If I'm rested

• Who I'm talking to (it's easier with familiar people)

• The intensity of the discussion

• Whether I'm already overstimulated when I enter the conversation

This shifting dynamic is a contributor to what I call my "people hangover." Just as someone can be hungover from drinking too much alcohol, I can feel hungover from making too much eye contact. And just like a traditional hangover, it often leaves me wondering why I pushed myself so hard in the first place.

But maybe I don't have to. I want to show that I'm paying attention, but does it have to be through eye contact?

Alternative Ways to Show Engagement

From a young age, I was taught to look people in the eye—"Look at me when I'm speaking to you!" But when I did, I was often told that my look was too intense or that I had a bad attitude because the way I did so didn't conform to societal norms. And in Western cultures, eye contact is often considered a sign that the listener is paying attention.

Over time, I developed tactics to demonstrate that I was paying attention in ways that worked for me, which often didn't involve eye contact. If eye contact is difficult for you, there are other ways to demonstrate engagement.

You don't need to hold eye contact to demonstrate you're paying attention.

Think of it as social judo—you're redirecting the energy away from eye contact and into more comfortable territory. And like any good martial art, it's about balance, not force. You can:

- **Be direct.** It's okay not to make eye contact. Simply say to the speaker that even though you're not making eye contact, you're paying attention, and then carry on in a way that is comfortable for you. "I'm listening carefully, even though my focus isn't on your eyes. Feel free to keep talking." (Bonus: This often makes the speaker feel more relaxed too.)

- **Try physical gestures.** Consider showing a range of physical signs, such as nodding your head, using relevant facial expressions, and using the thumbs-up gesture. It's amazing how far a well-timed thumbs-up can go in saying, "You've got my full attention."

- **Give verbal cues to show active listening.** Use verbal affirmations, such as "yes," or "that's interesting," or "I see what you mean." I find that when I say someone's name back to them in conversation ("that makes sense, Emily"), it's particularly effective. (And people love hearing their names— it's like a secret conversational handshake.)

While physical gestures and verbal cues can be effective on their own at demonstrating engagement, they're even more effective as complements to the direct approach.

Faking It (Also Known As Masking)

There are moments when blending in feels necessary. Whether it's a job interview, a family gathering, or a sensitive conversation, eye contact is often expected. We may push ourselves to meet that expectation—even if it's exhausting—because it makes others comfortable or helps us avoid unwanted attention.

While I don't force myself to make eye contact when I don't want to, there are times when I choose to do it. During the pandemic, when people's faces were covered with masks, I noticed I was compensating with stronger eye contact to read expressions more clearly. I felt that I needed to make direct eye contact, and for longer periods of time, to compensate for the loss.

If you find yourself needing to make direct eye contact, here are some suggestions that could make it more manageable:

- **Glance Away**—Who says you must hold and maintain eye contact for the duration of a conversation? Most neurotypicals don't. Instead, try making fleeting eye contact. Alternate between making eye contact and looking away before making eye contact again. It's about sharing a moment—not sharing every moment.

- **Briefly Close Your Eyes**—When asked a question, I might close my eyes to formulate a response, which naturally breaks eye contact. Most people interpret this as a sign of deep thought or concentration.

- **Focus Elsewhere on the Face**—An alternative to looking directly into someone's eyes is to focus on the area between their eyebrows. To the recipient, it appears as though you're looking at their eyes.

- **If You Wear Glasses or Sunglasses**—Allow your glasses to slide down your nose slightly to blur your vision and reduce the stress of maintaining eye contact. If safe to do so, you can also take your glasses off entirely and get a similar effect. And if you have the option in say, an outdoor setting, wearing sunglasses that obscure your eyes means the listeners can't see if you're making eye contact or not.

- **Choose Your Seat Strategically**—If you're speaking with someone in person, consider choosing side-by-side seating, a seat at an angle, and if possible, a seat with distractions, such as plants or a table between you and the person you're speaking with. I have a regular group meeting and one person in particular looks intensely at me whenever he's talking. I've learned to avoid sitting directly opposite him, which has proven quite effective.

You can practice these tactics with pets and close friends or relatives before attempting them in more high-stakes environments, such as in professional settings.

Applied Behavioral Analysis (ABA)

ABA was designed to teach social and communication skills, including eye contact, but it's controversial—and for good reason. It was originally built around making autistic people appear more "normal," often prioritizing neurotypical comfort over actual autistic needs.

In the past, that meant using punishment or negative reinforcement to push kids into behaviors that didn't come naturally. While modern ABA mostly relies on positive reinforcement, it still raises concerns.

For many families, ABA is one of the few therapy options available to them, and parents are often making the best choice they can with the resources they have. While I understand why parents may turn to ABA, I personally struggle with the idea that autistic traits should be trained away rather than supported.

When I first heard about ABA, I wondered if it would have helped me as a child. More likely, it would have pushed me to mask even more. Worse, it might have eroded my confidence, making me feel as if my natural tendencies were wrong.

But I'm learning that context matters. If ABA is used to push eye contact or suppress stimming—especially through coercion—I have deep concerns. But when it's used thoughtfully, to build essential life skills that support autonomy, safety, or communication—like learning to cross the street safely or ask for help when something feels wrong—it may offer value.

That's why I'm including this section—to encourage you to do your own research and decide what's right for you.

The Power of Looking Beyond the Eyes

Once I learned how to avoid eye contact—or to do so in ways I could manage—I realized the value of the other types of information I was able to gather instead, which helped me process the social cues that I would have otherwise missed. Now, I view this ability as one of my core strengths that enables me to assess people and their motives.

Processing social cues beyond eye contact has become one of my greatest strengths.

Instead of only looking at someone's eyes, I rely more heavily on other signals. Do a person's words match their body language? Do they tense up when discussing certain topics? What emphasis do they put on specific words?

I may not always immediately know what those cues mean, but I pattern-match and look for inconsistencies. I've gone from being scolded as an "insolent" child for the way I made eye contact to an adult who is often praised for having a good "picker," whether in people, in jobs, or in opportunities. This ability to pick up other important signals outside of eye contact gives me an edge in assessing situations and making well-informed choices.

Tool: Eye Contact Assessment and Strategy Builder

Eye Contact Comfort Assessment

This tool is designed to help you reflect on your comfort levels with eye contact in different situations. By identifying patterns, you can better understand when and why eye contact feels manageable or overwhelming, allowing you to develop strategies that work for you.

Instructions:

- Reflect on your recent interactions or typical scenarios.
- Rate your comfort level on a scale from 1 to 5:

    1: Very uncomfortable

    2: Somewhat uncomfortable

    3: Neutral

    4: Somewhat comfortable

    5: Very comfortable

- Note any triggers or factors that impact your rating.
- Use the additional prompts and strategy section below to develop actionable steps for managing eye contact more comfortably.

Scale Template

Scenario	Comfort Level (1–5)	Triggers/Comments
Making eye contact with close friends or family		Example: "I feel okay unless the topic is emotional or intense." •
Maintaining eye contact in small group discussions		Example: "I feel pressure to split my focus between everyone in the group." •
Holding eye contact in professional settings		Example: "Feels manageable if the conversation is casual, but stressful in interviews." •

Scenario	Comfort Level (1–5)	Triggers/Comments
Glancing at strangers in public settings		Example: "I avoid this because I'm worried they'll interpret it as confrontation." •
Making prolonged eye contact during intimate conversations		Example: "It feels too personal and like I'm exposed." •
Eye contact during public speaking		Example: "I look slightly over their heads because direct eye contact with an audience feels overwhelming." •
Situations with unpredictable interactions (e.g., networking)		Example: "I don't know where to look because I'm unsure of their expectations or reactions." •

Action Plan: Developing Strategies to Make Eye Contact More Comfortable

Use your Eye Contact Comfort Assessment results to identify patterns, triggers, and scenarios where eye contact feels easier or harder. For challenging situations, refer to earlier in the chapter for ideas on how you can adapt to mitigate the discomfort.

Scenario	Comfort Level (1–5)	Triggers/ Comments	Adaptation
Example: Maintaining eye contact in small group discussions	2	Example: "I feel pressure to split my focus between everyone in the group."	Alternate your gaze between different points in the group, such as focusing on the area between someone's eyebrows or glancing at a neutral spot like a table or an object in the room. Pair this with verbal affirmations ("That's a great point") to show engagement without the need for prolonged direct eye contact.

Scenario	Comfort Level (1–5)	Triggers/ Comments	Adaptation

Scenario	Comfort Level (1–5)	Triggers/ Comments	Adaptation

My Mind: What Looks Like Chaos Is Actually Order

Talking with me when I'm not masking—and sometimes even when I am—can feel like trying to piece together a story told in random order. Sudden changes of subject or unrelated thoughts might seem random or disjointed, but there's a system in the chaos—at least, from my perspective.

My mind works like one of those rotating lottery drums. As the balls swirl around inside, one will pop out unexpectedly, and I'll read it. I don't always control which ball pops out, but I'm aware of all the balls inside the drum (after all, I'm the one who put them there) and can keep track of them. Each ball represents a different idea or topic, which might seem disconnected to the person I'm talking to. What makes sense to me—because I can see the whole drum—might be hard for others to follow since they only see the ball that's popped out. This often means my conversations jump between seemingly unrelated topics, even though they're connected in my mind.

How My Brain Works

It's all tied to how my brain processes, organizes, and communicates information, a pattern that others on the spectrum might find familiar. Specifically, three things are happening:

- **Parallel Processing**

I'm **parallel processing** multiple ideas at once. This means that I can hold multiple thoughts in my mind simultaneously, shifting between them quickly. It's like having several tabs open on a browser, each running independently but all accessible to me at any time.

- **Associative Thinking**

The way one ball "pops out" reflects how my brain connects ideas. I excel at **associative thinking**—linking concepts in ways that might not seem obvious to others. These connections make perfect sense to me because I can see the entire drum. To someone without the same context or visibility, though, they might appear random or disconnected.

- **Hyperfocus and Awareness**

While juggling multiple thoughts, there are moments when one idea grabs my full attention—this is hyperfocus. When hyperfocus kicks in, I zero in on one "ball"—one thought—completely. At the same time, I'm still aware of the others swirling in the background, ready to jump to the next when needed. This allows me to engage deeply with one idea while still keeping track of the others.

I think it's pretty cool that I'm able to do this, but there is a downside: As I move to what may be perceived as random topics, people might think I'm not paying attention or that I'm bored with the conversation, when in fact, I'm usually neither. When this happens, I often say something like, "Placeholder, I'll come right back to that topic!" or "I'm paying attention but had another thought; I'll circle back to that!" Then I carry on and return to the original topic.

I view this way of processing as a huge net positive. While it may be messy, I wouldn't trade the way my brain works for anything. That said, not everyone experiences thinking this way. For some—such as those with ADHD or other neurological differences—their minds might feel less structured, more unpredictable, or work in entirely different ways. Each way of thinking brings its own strengths and challenges.

Maybe you approach conversations more linearly, keeping fewer "tabs" open at once. That might feel like the natural way to process, just as my swirling lottery drum feels natural to me.

What looks like chaos from the outside is simply a different kind of organization.

To others, my thinking may seem chaotic, but to me, it's not just order—it's a strength.

The Essentials:

Masking, Unmasking, and Finding Balance

- Masking is a tool, not an obligation—you decide when and where to use it.
- Balancing masking and unmasking is key—use it when it helps; let it go when it doesn't or if it starts feeling unhealthy.
- Not every reaction to how you present matters—focus on those who are important to you.
- Authentic connections happen when you can be yourself, even in small ways.
- Small, intentional steps make unmasking more manageable.
- The goal isn't to stop masking completely, but to reduce the strain.

Masking, Unmasking, and Finding Balance

The party was in high gear—a blur of people, noise, and overlapping conversations. I circled the room according to my social plan (see the chapter "Setting Yourself Up for Success at Social Gatherings" for more information), dropping in and out of groups with carefully rehearsed openers. I smiled, nodded, commented on someone's outfit, laughed at people's jokes, and maintained steady eye contact.

It looked effortless. It wasn't. And now my body was telling me that I needed to leave.

I activated my pre-determined exit strategy and was almost out the door when someone approached me to follow up on the career advice I'd casually mentioned earlier. At this point, my energy was flagging. My responses became shorter, forming complete sentences became a struggle, my smile faded, and I avoided eye contact more frequently.

He noticed. "Are you okay?"

Simply saying I was tired wouldn't have explained the breadth and depth of my responses; out of concern, I feared he'd seek help for me. I also wasn't comfortable sharing with him that I was autistic. Instead, I chose a simpler route:

"I'm an introvert and am just tired."

You can guess what came next.

"There's no way you're an introvert!"

His was a rational response based on the limited information he had of me. My outward friendliness and engagement contradicted the image of an introvert he likely held, and telling him I was only tired wouldn't have adequately explained my behavior. Had I told him I was autistic, I might still be with him at the party today answering questions! Fortunately, his disbelief faded quickly, and I escaped the conversation.

What I was doing has a name: masking.

Acting Neurotypical

Masking means hiding autistic traits to fit into social norms, often at the expense of one's emotional or physical well-being.

For me, masking feels like acting. I follow a social script—what I call *Natalie the Neurotypical*—that I've developed by observing others. This includes copying phrases and memorizing socially acceptable responses. At the same time, I suppress autistic traits like stimming. I force myself to make eye contact. I adjust my speech to sound engaged but not overly animated, always fine-tuning to fit expectations.

Masking can make interactions smoother—but it doesn't make me any less autistic.

Masking wasn't something I consciously decided to do. It started at an early age as I learned that playing a role could protect me. It felt like the social equivalent of wearing armor. I mask to protect myself from judgment, from being punished, and, most importantly, from being misunderstood.

But masking doesn't make me any less autistic—it just means I'm working hard to appear neurotypical. It requires continuous mental effort, which is one reason why it isn't sustainable. Like a muscle, if I overwork it, it needs time to recover.

The Cost of Masking

Masking helps me move through the world, but it comes at a cost—one I don't always recognize until it's too late. In the moment, I can push through, acting like my behavior is second nature. But when the mask comes off, I feel it: the exhaustion, the burnout, the weight of hours—or even days—spent performing as someone I'm not.

The fatigue isn't just physical. It's the mental strain of monitoring every social cue, suppressing natural instincts, and staying hyper-aware of how I'm presenting myself. It's the emotional weight of wondering if people actually like me—or just the version of me I've presented.

And sometimes, the hardest part isn't the effort itself—it's the recovery. After prolonged masking, I need time to reset, but the world doesn't always allow for that. So I push through, stretching myself thinner, until even basic interactions feel impossible.

I've learned to recognize the signs and pace myself. Some situations are worth masking for, and some aren't. It's not just about when I mask, but why.

I don't mask for everyone—
I choose when and where it's worth it.

Why I Mask

When I was in the fifth grade, I joined the school rocket club—the only girl in the group. I saved up my money to buy a rocket kit, and then spent months building it. On launch day, we ran out of time for mine. I was the only one who didn't get to launch, and when I complained to the group's advisor, I was told it didn't matter because I was a girl.

That night, I went home to my father, crying about how unfair it was. That's when he gave me some of the best advice of my life. He said, "There's something you need to understand. You're a girl, and because of that, you'll have to be twice as good as any boy to be seen as equal. You're right, it's not fair, but life's not fair. You have a choice. You can sit on the sidelines and let them decide that you don't belong, or you can stand up and decide your place in it."

The lesson my father taught me wasn't just about being a girl—it was about being different. I've carried that lesson into my life as an autistic person. I want to stay part of the world but without losing myself in it, and sometimes, masking helps me do that. Masking may not be fair, but it's something I control—a choice I make to stay engaged.

But that choice isn't always simple. Masking is effortful—but it's also *predictable*. I know the social rules and can guess the outcomes. Unmasking, on the other hand, introduces uncertainty. Will I be accepted? Will I have to explain myself? Sometimes, the energy cost of unmasking is higher than just maintaining the mask in the first place.

I've masked for so long that it has become automatic—hard to stop, but not impossible. And yet, here's the thing: I often choose not to.

Masking, on My Terms

Masking without losing myself is a balance, one I readily admit I haven't mastered. If the interaction is important, I may mask. If it isn't, I likely won't. I don't act for everyone; I use masking judiciously because of its significant downsides.

In the chapter "Setting Yourself Up for Success at Social Gatherings," I mentioned sitting behind the driver in a rideshare to avoid small talk. That's a conscious decision to conserve energy—one small way I avoid masking when I don't need to. Instead of masking all the time or never masking at all, balance means knowing when it serves me and when it doesn't.

For me, it's about making intentional choices: where to spend my energy, when to let the mask drop, and who gets to see the unfiltered version of me.

This balance isn't just about energy—it's about identity. If I spend so much of my time performing, what does that mean for my sense of self?

While there's the obvious physical and mental toll, an even greater concern is whether I'm ever truly myself or just an imitation of what others expect. Am I a fake? If I mask too much, does anyone truly know me?

How do I form genuine connections when so much of me is hidden?

Ultimately, how do I form genuine connections?

Creating Genuine Connections in Layers

While masking can create functional connections that allow for smoother interactions, it rarely allows for authentic connections—the kind that actually sustain me instead of drain me.

Relationships are a gradual process of self-disclosure that is built in layers. Trust, understanding, and authenticity develop over time, often starting with small talk and then gradually deepening with familiarity and frequency.

I apply the same steps to unmasking. I test the waters—small disclosures, subtle shifts in how I interact—and watch how people respond. Do they accept the real me, or do they only engage when I'm mirroring them? Do I feel more comfortable, or does it just add another layer of exhaustion?

When unmasking feels right, it strengthens the connection. When it doesn't, I take that as useful information too. Either way, I'm learning who accepts me—and who doesn't.

3 Steps to Shift From Performance to Authenticity

The goal isn't to eliminate masking overnight—it's to find a balance that lets you engage while protecting your well-being and sense of self. To begin, experiment with these three steps:

1.   Identify the Right Spaces.

Start with low-risk, low-stakes environments where the pressure to perform is minimal. This could be casual meetups with friends, online spaces like forums or interest-based groups where text-based communication offers more control, or hobbies where shared interests naturally facilitate connection. A high-stakes situation like an important presentation? Save that for when you've built up your comfort level.

2.   Experiment with Gradual Unmasking.

Reduce energy-draining behaviors first. For the biggest impact in the shortest time, start with the behaviors that drain you the most and work your way down from there. Think about what masking characteristic is the most difficult for you. If maintaining **eye contact** is exhausting, allow yourself to break it more often. If **small talk** is draining, keep responses brief instead of overexplaining. If suppressing fidgeting is tiring, introduce small, subtle **stims**—like tapping a pen, adjusting jewelry, or bouncing a foot.

Use authentic communication styles. Try responding in ways that feel natural to you. If you usually filter your excitement about a special interest, experiment with sharing a little more enthusiasm. If you tend to script responses, allow a moment of spontaneity.

Test out directness in communication. If masking means softening your opinions or mimicking social niceties, try being slightly more direct with a trusted person and observe the response.

Notice reactions, but prioritize how *you* feel. Instead of assuming others won't accept your unmasked self, test it. Do they engage with you differently? Do you feel more comfortable? Pay attention to whether unmasking in certain ways makes socializing easier or harder. If you're unsure what your unmasked self feels like, you're not alone. Long-term masking can blur that awareness. The goal isn't instant clarity but slow, intentional exploration.

3. **Build comfort with reactions.** One of the most exhausting aspects of unmasking is the fear of how others will respond. Reframing this can help:

- **Not every reaction matters.** If a stranger at a party doesn't like your communication style, does it really affect your life?

- **Discomfort doesn't mean rejection.** Sometimes, people just need time to adjust.

- **Not everyone will connect deeply—and that's okay.** True relationships emerge with those who value you as you are.

If being yourself pushes someone away,
that tells you all you need to know.

Over time, you'll begin recognizing when it's safe to be yourself and when it's not worth the effort.

How to Tell If Unmasking Isn't the Right Move (Right Now)

Pay attention to how you're feeling. If unmasking leaves you more drained than energized, leads to persistent negative reactions, or compromises your sense of safety, it's fine to step back.

These are experiments—if one doesn't "work," that doesn't mean it was a failure! You're gathering information and trying new things. Choosing to pause is a strategic choice rather than a setback. Some situations and people will be better suited for unmasking than others, and that's valuable to know.

Unmasking should be a process of self-revelation, not self-defense. If it starts feeling like the latter, you can always step back. Then, when you're ready, try again in spaces that feel safer, with people who are genuinely interested in knowing you beyond the surface.

What If You Can't Stop Masking?

Masking was my default for years, and I didn't even realize I was doing it. Once I realized it, letting go of a lifelong habit wasn't easy. There's no easy "off switch" that allowed me to instantly stop masking, and the task felt nearly impossible. Over time, it was a gradual process of recognizing where

I was expending unnecessary energy and where I could allow myself to unmask—bit by bit.

If fully unmasking feels overwhelming, start small. Focus on manageable shifts rather than an all-or-nothing approach. In some environments, especially professional or high-stakes situations, masking may still be necessary. The goal isn't to eliminate it completely, but to reduce the strain where you can and reclaim spaces where you don't need to perform.

Some days, masking will be the easier choice, and some days unmasking will. There's no right way to do this—only what works for you.

The goal isn't perfection—it's reducing the weight of performance where you can.

Making Peace with Masking

Masking is a complex, deeply personal choice.

The goal isn't to stop masking entirely or force yourself into a version of authenticity that doesn't feel safe. Instead, it's about understanding when masking serves you and when it doesn't—so you can make choices that support your well-being.

Unmasking is a decision to show up as you are, not to meet someone else's comfort level. It's about reclaiming your energy, your comfort, and your right to exist without constant performance. Who deserves to see the real you? That's a decision only you can make.

This isn't about becoming more palatable to the world—it's about making space for who you are to exist in it. Finding that balance is an ongoing process, shaped by intentional choice, self-acceptance, and the freedom to engage on your own terms.

Recognizing your unmasked self doesn't mean becoming someone new—it means rediscovering who you've always been.

∴ **Tool:** Unmasking Support Pack

- **Am I Masking?**

- **Where Do You Mask the Most?**

- **Low-Risk Unmasking Experiments**

- **Recognizing Your Unmasked Self**

Part 1: Am I Masking?

Masking can be so automatic that it's hard to recognize it in yourself. This checklist helps you explore whether you're masking in different situations by identifying common masking behaviors. It isn't about judging whether masking is "good" or "bad"—it's simply a tool to help you notice patterns.

Recognize how you adapt.

Check off any statements that feel familiar.

Speech & Communication:

☐ I rehearse what I want to say before speaking, even in casual conversations.

☐ I mimic other people's speech patterns, tone, or slang to fit in.

☐ I force myself to use small talk, even when I find it pointless or exhausting.

☐ I consciously modulate my voice (e.g., making it sound more expressive or avoiding monotone).

☐ I soften or filter my directness to avoid making others uncomfortable.

Body Language & Eye Contact:

☐ I force myself to make eye contact, even when it feels unnatural or uncomfortable.

☐ I monitor my facial expressions to match the expected reaction in conversations.

- ☐ I suppress stimming (e.g., fidgeting, tapping, rocking) to appear more "normal."
- ☐ I consciously control my posture and gestures to seem more natural.
- ☐ I copy other people's body language as a way to blend in.

Social Expectations & Energy Management:
- ☐ I script or pre-plan responses to avoid awkward pauses.
- ☐ I laugh or smile when I don't actually find something funny, just to maintain the flow of conversation.
- ☐ I feel like I'm performing a role rather than just being myself in social settings.
- ☐ I mentally track social "rules" while interacting with people.
- ☐ I force myself to stay in social situations even when I'm drained, just to avoid seeming rude.

Emotional Expression & Regulation:
- ☐ I hold back excitement or enthusiasm about my interests to avoid seeming "too much."
- ☐ I mimic other people's emotions so they don't think I'm indifferent.
- ☐ I avoid talking about certain topics because I've learned people find them odd or uninteresting.
- ☐ I suppress my reactions to sensory discomfort (e.g., pretending bright lights or loud sounds don't bother me).
- ☐ I exaggerate my enthusiasm or expressions so people don't think I'm uninterested or rude.
- ☐ I feel like I have different "versions" of myself for different situations.

Part 2: Where Do You Mask the Most?

Masking can look different in different settings. This reflection helps you notice where masking feels most automatic or effortful. Find a quiet moment to reflect on your daily interactions. Think about a typical day or a specific recent interaction and answer the following:

1. **Where was I?** (e.g., work, a social event, family gathering, online, etc.)

_____

_____

_____

_____

2. **Did I feel the need to adjust how I spoke, moved, or reacted? If so, in what ways?**

_____

_____

_____

_____

3. **What was my reason for masking?** (e.g., to fit in, to avoid conflict, to be polite, to stay safe, or another reason)

_____

_____

_____

4. **How did it feel?** (e.g., *exhausting, neutral, helpful*)

_____

_____

_____

_____

5. **Would I want to adjust how much I mask in this situation next time?**

_____

_____

_____

_____

Part 3: Low-Risk Unmasking Experiments

Trying to unmask in all areas of life at once can feel impossible—but you don't have to. Start small. This tool helps you experiment with unmasking in low-risk ways, giving you space to reflect on what feels right for you.

Step 1: Choose an Area to Experiment In

Pick one small aspect of masking that you want to adjust. Some ideas:

- ☐ Letting yourself stim slightly instead of suppressing it
- ☐ Reducing eye contact when it feels uncomfortable
- ☐ Speaking in your natural cadence instead of mirroring others
- ☐ Allowing yourself a break from social scripting
- ☐ Letting your enthusiasm for a topic show

Step 2: Choose a Low-Stakes Setting

Try unmasking in a situation where you feel safe or where the stakes are minimal. Some examples:

- With a trusted friend who already understands you
- In a text conversation, where you have more control over responses
- At home, where you can practice in private before trying it socially
- In a casual setting, like a coffee shop or online forum
- In an environment where you're anonymous

Step 3: Reflect on the Experience

After your experiment, take a moment to process:

1. What did you try?

_____

_____

_____

_____

2. How did it feel while doing it? (e.g., awkward, freeing, exhausting, neutral)

_____

_____

_____

_____

3. How did others react? (Did they notice? Was it a non-issue?)

_____

_____

_____

_____

4. Would you want to try it again? Why or why not?

_____

_____

_____

_____

5. What's one other small change you'd like to try next time?

_____

_____

_____

_____

Regardless of the outcome, acknowledge that trying something different is a step forward. What did you learn about yourself in the process?

Part 4: Recognizing Your Unmasked Self

For many autistic people, masking becomes so automatic that the idea of unmasking feels vague or unfamiliar. If you've spent years adapting to social expectations, you might not even know what "unmasked" looks or feels like for you. This section helps you explore your natural traits and preferences.

Step 1: Reflect on When You Feel Most at Ease

Think about times when you feel most comfortable and unfiltered. This might be when you're alone, engaging in a favorite activity, or with people who accept you fully.

- When do I feel most relaxed and free to be myself?

_____

_____

_____

_____

- What activities bring me comfort and joy without effort?

_____

_____

_____

_____

- Are there people I feel completely at ease around? Who are they?

_____

_____

_____

_____

- How does my body feel in these moments? (e.g., less tension, easier breathing, natural movement)

_____

_____

_____

_____

Step 2: Notice What Feels Different

Compare these moments of ease to times when you're masking. Ask yourself:

- Do I communicate differently when I'm fully comfortable?

_____

_____

_____

_____

- How does my voice, tone, or pacing change?

_____

_____

_____

_____

- Do I stim more naturally when I'm alone or with trusted people?

_____

_____

_____

_____

- Are my emotions or expressions different when I'm not monitoring myself?

_____

_____

_____

_____

Step 3: Experiment with Small Moments of Unmasking

Unmasking doesn't have to be an all-or-nothing shift. Try noticing and embracing small moments where you naturally drop the mask:

- ☐ Letting yourself stim without suppressing it
- ☐ Speaking in your natural cadence instead of mirroring others
- ☐ Expressing excitement without filtering it down
- ☐ Giving yourself permission to pause instead of scripting responses
- ☐ Spending time alone to reconnect with your natural rhythms

Step 4: Trust That Self-Discovery Takes Time

You may be unsure of what your unmasked self feels like yet. Long-term masking can blur that awareness, and unlearning it isn't immediate. You don't have to force it—just observe what feels right.

Trying something different is a win. What did you learn about yourself in the process? What patterns or preferences did you notice? Were there any surprises?

Ask yourself: How can I optimize for more situations where I can unmask and be myself?

Masking vs. Social Learning

I was catching up with a friend who is a therapist, when she mentioned that many of her clients are struggling with social learning—observing and adopting behaviors to navigate social environments—and questioning whether they may be autistic. Intrigued, I asked her to explain the difference. She paused for a moment and then said, *"It comes down to why someone is adjusting their behavior."*

Masking, she explained, involves suppressing or concealing autistic traits to fit in and avoid judgment. It often stems from societal pressure and can lead to exhaustion or burnout.

Social learning, on the other hand, is about growth and understanding—choosing to adopt certain behaviors to connect better or participate more effectively. While masking can leave a person feeling disconnected, social learning is more likely to feel empowering because it enhances communication and relationships while allowing for personal authenticity.

Key Differences:

- **Masking** is about concealing autistic traits, while **social learning** expands skill sets without suppressing identity.

- **Masking** requires constant monitoring and self-adjustment, while **social learning** becomes more intuitive over time.

- **Masking** often leads to burnout and loss of self-awareness, while **social learning** fosters connection without compromising identity.

Most people naturally adjust their behavior in social situations, learning what works and refining their approach over time. But there's a difference between developing social skills and constantly monitoring yourself to perform acceptably.

For many neurotypicals, adjusting behavior in social situations happens with less conscious effort—it's often a background process rather than something they have to actively monitor.

In contrast, autistic people often engage in constant, deliberate self-checks.

"Am I making appropriate eye contact?"
"Is my body language signaling what I want it to?"
"Is my stimming noticeable?"

While masking can leave a person feeling disconnected, drained, or like they're "performing," social learning is more likely to feel empowering—helping you connect in a way that still feels like you.

The difference isn't just about discomfort—learning any new skill can feel awkward.

Instead, ask yourself: Am I adjusting to connect more effectively, or am I suppressing myself to avoid judgment?

Social learning allows for growth, while masking demands performance. The goal isn't to force yourself to be someone you're not—it's to build skills while staying true to who you are.

The Essentials:

Taking Control and Making Meetings Work for You

- Preparation reduces stress—where appropriate, ask for an agenda, materials, or a facilitator to help meetings feel structured.

- Define your own goals for the meeting alongside the host's objectives.

- Meetings can be a chance to influence outcomes, not just a task to endure.

- Use small actions, like asking about next steps, to keep meetings productive.

- It's okay not to know everything—thoughtful follow-ups can make a stronger impression.

- Accepting that some meetings might feel unproductive for you but valuable for others can reduce your stress significantly.

Taking Control and Making Meetings Work for You

The email notification popped up on my screen:

Invitation: Team Brainstorming Meeting — Fri, Jan 12 @ 11:00 a.m. — 12:00 p.m. (EST)

My pulse quickened. A brainstorming meeting, about what? What did I need to prepare? Without more information, would I be able to contribute effectively? Brainstorming sessions always felt chaotic to me, with unstructured discussions and unclear goals. Anxiety crept in.

This was my usual response to meeting invites, but it wasn't just brainstorming sessions that were stressful—it was any gathering where I felt uncertain about the expectations.

This was a huge problem. I enjoyed the other aspects of my work, but I recognized that without participating in meetings, I couldn't do that work effectively. I needed to collaborate with other departments, have a back-and-forth dialogue to solve problems, and, importantly, I needed to be in the meeting room or I would lose my voice to influence decisions and outcomes.

With a little preparation, a dreaded meeting can become an opportunity to make your voice heard and to influence outcomes.

I eventually learned to break down the act of meetings into three more manageable steps that made the process less overwhelming, less intimidating, and more structured: before the meeting, during the meeting, and after the meeting.

Before the Meeting

My previous inclination when preparing for a meeting was to run through as many scenarios as I could imagine and practice how to respond. It was exhausting and often a waste of time due to the limited information available.

Now, I proactively reach out to the host in advance of the meeting and ask:

- **For an agenda, if there isn't one and it's a larger or formal meeting.** Given my personality, this can be a bit tricky, as I can come across as judgmental. I frame my request by sharing that I want to be prepared and helpful in the discussion. I often find that the host is earlier in their career and may not yet have fully developed their professional skills; they are generally appreciative of the assist. It's rare that I have to ask the same host again for an agenda for subsequent meetings because they later see how much more we get done with a bit of advance preparation.

- **What are the top two-three things they would like to get out of the meeting, again, so that I can be supportive of what they're trying to accomplish.** If there isn't an agenda (or even if there is one), having a quick, informal discussion about the host's goals helps set a positive tone for our forward interaction, as we're now a team working to accomplish the same things.

- **If there are any materials I should read in advance to prepare for the meeting.** I frequently have my best ideas once I've had a chance to think on a subject without the pressure that often comes from being in a meeting, but not all meetings have advance materials. In those cases, I pattern-match by searching old emails and notes on similar subjects as preparation.

- **To include a facilitator.** If the meeting doesn't have an agenda, it likely doesn't have a facilitator, since that's part of a facilitator's role. Even if there is an agenda, if the meeting is large enough, I may still suggest we include a facilitator. This helps keep the meeting focused, ensures that we cover all the necessary points, and respects everyone's time. I emphasize that this isn't about control but about making the meeting more efficient and effective for everyone involved.

In addition, I think through what I want to get out of the meeting. Let's say we're discussing a new project. I might consider what role I'd like to play or try to better understand a particular part of the project and how it impacts my department. This is my true, most important prep. Just as I want to help meet the host's goals, I want to meet my own as well.

During the Meeting

You know the agenda, understand what the host wants to accomplish at the meeting, and have your own goals in mind—you're prepared and ready to contribute. Now, consider these additional tips during the meeting to make it more productive and manageable:

- **If no one is taking notes, suggest that someone should.** If no one volunteers, consider doing it yourself. To avoid being seen as the permanent note-taker (often a career killer), I offer to take notes with the understanding that we rotate the responsibility at future meetings.

- **Instead of waiting to be asked a question or remaining silent throughout the meeting, proactively contribute something to the meeting to highlight the value you provide.** It can be an observation, a question, or a suggestion. An added benefit is that if notes are taken, there will be a record of your contribution.

Every meeting is an opportunity to highlight your value—this is your time to shine.

- **If staying still, calm, and focused is challenging, consider options like doodling, standing (which provides an opportunity for rocking), or stretching.** For longer meetings, I might take a break and go to the restroom.

- **By the end of the meeting, if there are no clear next steps, ask the group what they should be.** This is another chance to demonstrate your contribution with a relatively low level of effort.

- **As a follow-on to my question of next steps, I request meeting action items with assigned responsibilities and timelines.** I'm frequently surprised by people's reactions when I ask this question. It's often seen as a novelty. For many, the discussion itself seems to be the point of the meeting, whereas for me, it's merely the vehicle for getting things done. I remind myself that just as I want others to respect my working style, I need to respect theirs. Sometimes you'll just have to sit through meetings that feel like a waste of time to you but that are helpful to others. Accepting this has significantly reduced my stress level around meetings.

- **It's a fallacy that you need to know the answer to every question posed to you, even if it's in your area of expertise.** If I don't know, I might say, "Good question. Can I get back to you on that?" I then follow up promptly and ask that the answer be included in the meeting minutes, if there are any. You can't take this approach every time, but it's an additional tactic you can deploy strategically.

It's okay to say, "Let me get back to you." Thoughtful follow-ups matter more than instant answers.

After the Meeting

The meeting is over—you're done, almost. There are a few more steps needed to translate the effort you already spent into results:

- **If there are notes, read them thoroughly.** With my attention to detail, I often catch errors, and it shows that I'm paying attention. I will then gently let the host know or inform the entire distribution list if that is more appropriate.

- **Promptly follow-up on action items, if you have them.** If follow-up isn't needed immediately, I set electronic reminders for myself to follow-up at a later date.

- **Reflect.** Ask yourself: Were my goals met? If not, consider how you might adjust your approach for the next meeting, and then make changes accordingly. I also reflect on the host's meeting style. If it worked for me, I might go out of my way to work with them again. If it didn't, I might attempt to minimize the number of their meetings I attend. Where possible, gravitate toward the leaders whose style works for you.

- **Check in with a trusted colleague.** I want to add value and push people a bit out of their comfort zones without becoming "that person," but I may not be able to read the warning signs. If I go overboard and alienate myself from the team, I may be left out of future meetings and undercut my and the team's effectiveness. I find that a quick check-in with a trusted co-worker is an excellent way to get feedback on the team's perception of how things are going.

Checking in with a trusted colleague can help you gauge how your approach is being received.

You might have noticed that many of these tactics put the burden on you, which can be exhausting. I try to strike a balance. Pick and choose what works for you, and be willing to take small steps for incremental improvement.

You might also have noticed that many of these tactics—agendas, meeting minutes, action items—are basic meeting hygiene that is helpful to the company too. What I need to be productive is also what the company needs to be productive—we're aligned.

Advice to managers: If you want to operate efficiently and meet company goals, hire people on the spectrum! We can bring diverse skills, offer a fresh perspective, and help teams operate more efficiently and effectively.

Once I developed meeting tactics and strategies, I had more energy to use productively. In time, I became the person meeting participants sought input from when they wanted new ideas or a detailed understanding of a topic.

I went from dreading meetings to feeling good about my contributions to the point that I now prefer to lead meetings instead of only participating. It has also given me the confidence to take on more leadership roles and influence outcomes more directly.

So far, we've focused on in-person meetings, but many meetings today are held virtually. While some of the steps are the same for in-person versus virtual meetings—such as having an agenda, taking notes, and following up on action items—virtual meetings have their own unique considerations. Please read ahead to the next chapter to learn more.

⠇ **Tool:** Smart Meeting Planner

Not all meetings require the same level of preparation. Use this planner flexibly: Complete it fully for high-stakes meetings or rely on the Quick Start Guide for a streamlined approach to stay organized and maintaining good meeting habits.

Quick-Start Guide

If you're short on time or don't need the full planner, focus on these key questions:

*   What is the purpose of this meeting?

_____

_____

_____

_____

*   What are my top 2 – 3 goals?

_____

_____

_____

_____

- **ACTION: Do I need to prepare anything (agenda, materials, questions)?**

_____

_____

_____

_____

- **What's my role in the meeting?**

_____

_____

_____

_____

- **What are the next steps after the meeting?**

_____

_____

_____

_____

If you have more time or need deeper preparation, proceed to the detailed sections below for comprehensive meeting planning.

Meeting Preparation

Meeting Details

o   Date and Time: _____

o   Host: _____

o   Meeting Type (Brainstorm, Status Update, Planning, etc.):

_____

o   Meeting Venue (Virtual, Conference Room, Small Office):

_____

Preparation Checklist

o   Have I requested or reviewed an agenda?

o   What are my goals for the meeting?

   1.   _____

   2.   _____

   3.   _____

o   Have I clarified what the host wants to achieve? What are their goals?

   1.   _____

   2.   _____

   3.   _____

○   Have I reviewed any materials provided or gathered my own relevant notes?

○   Have I prepared any questions or observations to share during the meeting?

1. _____

2. _____

Role and Contribution

My Role in This Meeting:

○   Decision-maker

○   Contributor

○   Observer

○   Other: _____

Key Contribution(s):

○   What is my primary input or insight for this meeting?

▪   _____

▪   _____

○   Do I have any challenges or questions I'd like to address?

▪   _____

Engagement Strategy:

○   How will I demonstrate my engagement? (e.g., verbal affirmations, asking questions, note-taking)

▪   _____

Post-Meeting Reflection

Complete this section after the meeting to track your impact and identify areas for growth.

Reflection Questions:

o   Were my personal goals achieved?

- Yes
- Partially
- No
- What will I do differently next time?

_____

_____

o   Were the host's goals achieved?

- Yes
- Partially
- No
- What steps can I take to better support their objectives in the future?

_____

_____

What Worked Well That I'll Build On:

o   _____

o   _____

What I Will Do to Improve Next Time:

o   _____

o   _____

Action Items:

o   What are my next steps?

   ▪   _____

   ▪   _____

o   Who else needs follow-up?

   ▪   _____

   ▪   _____

Feedback Opportunity:

o   Did I check in with a trusted colleague about my contributions or team dynamics?

   ▪   Yes
   ▪   No
   ▪   Notes from feedback:

_____

_____

_____

_____

_____

_____

_____

The Essentials:

8 Tactics for Better Virtual Meetings

- Virtual meetings offer flexibility and reduce environmental impact but come with unique challenges like social cue gaps, technical issues, and challenges processing overlapping stimuli.

- Good meeting hygiene applies to both in-person and virtual meetings but requires specific adjustments in the online setting.

- Leverage virtual meeting tools like reaction emojis, raised-hand icons, and private chat to clarify communication and avoid interruptions.

- Prepare small talk topics in advance for smoother meeting openings, especially for smaller virtual gatherings.

- While not without their difficulties, virtual meetings give you control to create a setup that works for you.

8 Tactics for Better Virtual Meetings

Earlier in my career, I commuted from San Francisco up to ninety minutes one way to work in Silicon Valley, only to turn around at the end of the day and do it all over again in the reverse direction, at least five days a week. This meant spending 180 minutes a day gripping the steering wheel of my car in white-knuckled fear, navigating Highway 101 during bumper-to-bumper rush hour traffic. Now, with remote work more commonly accepted and the advent of virtual meetings, I've been able to reclaim that commute time. What a relief!

While virtual meetings offer flexibility and help the environment by reducing the carbon footprint, they're not without their own set of challenges. To begin, the lack of in-person interaction can make it harder to read social cues and gauge reactions. The unpredictability of sudden technical issues can cause stress and anxiety, and background noise and overlapping voices can be difficult to process and filter out.

These are on top of the challenges that already exist from meetings in general. Still, for me, it's a big net positive.

Fortunately, many of the same meeting tactics for in-person meetings we discussed in the previous chapter apply to virtual meetings, but new ones are also needed to adapt to the new technology and medium.

Virtual meetings build on the same foundations as in-person ones but require specific adjustments to stay effective.

Here are eight more strategies to help you manage virtual meetings specifically:

1. **Arrange your physical space.** If you have concurrent meetings with someone in your home or office, plan in advance where each person will take theirs to avoid dueling meetings. Ensure you are not backlit by the sun or facing it directly. Use a chair that is comfortable enough for the duration of the meeting.

2. **Reduce visual stimuli.** Turn off email alerts and other unnecessary notifications, limit the number of open tabs and windows on your screen, and use a simplified computer background. Hide non-talking meeting participants by using speaker view instead of gallery view.

3. **Optimize audio quality.** Implement a "mute when not speaking" rule to minimize background noise. Use noise-canceling headphones or earbuds to reduce echo and feedback. If possible, remind participants to avoid typing or shuffling papers near their microphones. Provide a transcript of the meeting.

Clarity in communication is key—
virtual tools like captions and transcripts
help everyone stay on the same page.

4. **Test Wi-Fi, audio, and visual technologies before the meeting begins.** Have a backup plan in case of technical failures, adjust your camera angle and lighting—even if you choose to keep them off—and join the meeting a few minutes early to resolve any issues. Perform a final sound and video check with participants before the meeting starts to confirm quality.

5. **Have a conversation starter ready.** Except in cases of large virtual meetings, most meetings start with small talk before the meeting officially begins. Be ready to share where you're calling from (one of the most common questions asked), any vacation or holiday plans, what you did over the weekend, or what you're going to do in the coming weekend. Come prepared with small talk to contribute.

6. **Leverage medium-specific communication tools.** Use reaction emojis to express emotions clearly, and employ a structured system for speaking, like using the "hands up" icon or raising hands physically to indicate a desire to speak. Utilize private messaging to communicate directly with the host or other participants for specific points or clarifications. *Note that some organizations may use different platforms or systems, so adapt these suggestions to fit your specific context.*

7. **Experiment with eye contact strategies.** Disable the screen's self-view

feature to focus on the meeting content instead of yourself, look at the speaker's forehead or mouth and not directly into their eyes, and position your camera at eye level, looking at it occasionally to simulate eye contact without maintaining it constantly. Alternate your focus between different areas of the screen and the camera to give your eyes a break and reduce the strain of constant eye contact.

8. **Boost information processing.** Record meetings so you can later review the information at your own pace. Enable captions to help interpret visual cues and follow along more easily. Take breaks during long meetings. If materials are shared in advance via screen-sharing, review them beforehand to reduce reliance on live visuals. Then, during the meeting, follow along on your own copy—either on a separate screen or printed out if that's easier. Ask to keep your video off if it helps reduce anxiety.

Virtual meetings come with challenges, but they also let you design an environment that works best for you—boosting both productivity and comfort.

It's possible that even with these tactics, you'll be unable to participate in virtual meetings from time to time. If that happens, read the notes and follow up with the meeting organizer or a colleague to catch up on any missed information and ask any questions you may have. Then, think through what you might want to change next time to fully participate in meetings.

It's funny, but after learning these tools, I now prefer virtual meetings over in-person. They allow me to manage my energy better, and participate in ways that feel more comfortable and productive.

And I admit that, yes, I do like that I can wear pajama bottoms and no one knows it but me.

⠔ **Tool:** Smart Virtual Meeting Planner

This planner complements the **Smart Meeting Planner** from the previous chapter. While many principles apply to both in-person and virtual meetings, this version focuses on adjustments specific to virtual settings. This planner is merely a guide—feel free to adapt it to suit your specific needs, meeting styles, and preferences.

TASK	NOTES
• Have I tested my tech? (Wi-Fi, camera, microphone, platform login)	
• Is my physical setup ready? (Lighting, seating, background distractions)	

TASK	NOTES
• Have I minimized on-screen distractions? (Closed unnecessary tabs, set notifications to Do Not Disturb)	
• Am I prepared for small talk? (Think about a quick update, weekend plans, or a light topic to share)	
• What virtual tools can I use to communicate better? (Emojis, "hands up," private chat)	
• Do I have a backup plan for tech issues? (Phone numbers, alternative platform links)	

Why Might Autism Feel More Intense as We Age?

I was speaking with a colleague when he mentioned that I didn't seem like myself. "Is everything okay?" he asked. His question struck me as odd because I felt completely like myself. I assured him that I was fine—great, even—but as the conversation continued, I started noticing his physical reactions to what I said. His face shifted through a range of emotions: surprise, confusion, and even irritation.

I couldn't figure out what had changed, and then it hit me: I usually masked with this person. In fact, masking with him had become second nature—it wasn't a conscious decision—but for some reason I had stopped. I began having similar experiences with others. My usual tools no longer felt adequate. It made me wonder, was my autism becoming more acute? Why was I no longer able to mask?

Does autism intensify with age?

Same Autism, Different Life Experiences

No, autism doesn't become more severe with age—it's not a progressive condition. I was born autistic, and I'll always be autistic. But how I experience it can change based on life's circumstances and the tools I develop.

In some situations, life may feel easier, and in some, it may feel more difficult, but my autism remains constant.

Why It May *Feel* Harder Over Time

Life can become challenging as we age, regardless of neurotype, but for someone who is autistic, these challenges might feel magnified, giving the illusion that autism itself is intensifying. For me, the number-one driver is autistic burnout. It's years of accumulated masking, sensory overload, and living in a world that wasn't built for me all catching up at once, leaving less capacity to manage new demands.

Burnout doesn't make autism more intense—it just makes it harder to manage the same challenges I've always faced. It's not that my sensory sensitivities or social difficulties have worsened; it's that my reserves to handle them have diminished.

But there are other factors too, such as greater self-awareness, the added pressures of "adulting," changing energy levels, health issues, and for women, perimenopause and menopause. These all add new demands that stretch an already limited capacity.

Together, these cumulative pressures may create the perception that one's autism is becoming more acute. In reality, it's the weight of life's demands on a reduced capacity that makes it feel harder.

Thankfully, while some things in life become more difficult, other aspects feel more manageable because of the experience and tools I've gained over the years.

Why It May *Feel* Easier Over Time

A few months ago, I dined at a restaurant I normally avoided because it was too loud, despite loving the food. This time, I enjoyed myself. Even with the animated exchanges around me, I could have a conversation with my dining companion. Why was this possible now? Then I realized: Aha, I'm wearing noise-canceling earphones!

Technology, like my earphones, has made my life easier, but so has understanding my needs. Over time, I've learned my triggers and how to avoid them, and I've created tools that work for me.

But the single biggest factor making life easier is self-acceptance. This didn't come overnight. For years, I felt like I had to prove myself—proving that I was capable, proving that I could "fit in," proving that I could meet neurotypical expectations, even if it drained me.

Self-acceptance started small. I allowed myself to set boundaries without apology, like saying no to events that overwhelmed me or taking breaks when I needed them.

Then it grew: I didn't have to be perfect, just myself. When I stopped spending so much energy pretending, I could then invest that energy into things I loved—my work, my relationships, and myself.

I try my best, but when I fail, I still take responsibility for my actions (I make amends when I unintentionally hurt someone). I also remind myself that I'm a decent person. I make mistakes and can do dumb things, but at the end of the day, I give myself the benefit of the doubt.

The older I get, the more I relax and find ways to work with my brain, rather than against it.

The Essentials:

One Autistic's Approach to Leadership

- Being autistic doesn't mean you can't lead—you can, but in your own way while supporting your team.

- Focus on the team's goals, not enforcing your process or method.

- Create space for self-reviews to uncover unspoken feedback you may have missed.

- Take regular "laps" around the office to acknowledge and engage with your team casually.

- Build a flexible leadership toolkit that works for all team members, neurodiverse or neurotypical.

One Autistic's Approach to Leadership

I Had Found My Niche

In the technology world, where precision and unconventional thinking are valued, the mix of exactness and creativity played to my strengths. I gravitated toward engineering and operations, where I was one of the few women on the team—and sometimes the only woman. What might have seemed odd to others was often chalked up to my gender. In a male-dominated field, my "otherness" was explained away as part of being a woman rather than recognized as traits of autism.

My autism largely went unnoticed, but it shaped both my work and my leadership style. I went from being an individual contributor to leading teams of hundreds of people. I've worked across countries, time zones, languages, and cultures. Throughout, I've leveraged the strengths of my autism and learned to adapt it to the varying demands of my position.

Just as in a medical environment where the doctor's focus is on meeting the needs of a patient, in a leadership role I needed to support and motivate my team. To help my team succeed, I had to refine my communication—offering support and encouragement in ways that worked for them. I worked on practicing active listening, adjusting my social interactions, and recognizing and celebrating achievements—skills that didn't come naturally to me. These areas were like muscles I needed to strengthen.

Where I could adapt, I did. And where I couldn't, I didn't. I accepted that some aspects of my autism would always be present and stopped trying to change them just to fit in.

By understanding the specific challenges I faced and developing strategies and tools to address them, I tried to turn my perceived "otherness" to my advantage. My need for structure and predictability led me to implement highly organized management systems, which improved team efficiency and clarity. My attention to detail and pattern-matching allowed me to spot potential issues early.

I wasn't always a good leader—not even close. And here's where I think I'm not so different from my neurotypical peers: We're all works in progress, trying to figure things out, and we each bring different traits to our roles. While there are areas where I struggled and my peers didn't, there are also areas where they struggled and I excelled.

Being autistic doesn't disqualify you from leading—
it just means you may lead differently.
And that's not a bad thing.

Another area where autistics and neurotypicals are similar is that just as autistics may not want to be leaders, there are neurotypicals who don't want to be leaders either. **Simply being autistic doesn't automatically mean that you're unfit to serve in this role if you want to.** With this in mind, it's important to consider some of the leadership challenges that autistic individuals may encounter, along with possible tactics to mitigate them.

Common Leadership Challenges for Autistics

Lack of Patience

It happened during a Monday morning team meeting. As a highly competent team member gave his verbal report, I interrupted several times. Eventually, he gave up. Later, we met privately, and he asked why I kept interrupting; he found it disrespectful. I hadn't meant to be rude, but he was right—I struggled to control my impatience. It was the first time I realized that I was an interrupter.

Some autistic individuals (myself included) process information quickly. This can lead to frustration when others don't immediately grasp our perspective. But given time, most people do—if we let them process at their own pace.

- After sharing an idea or instruction, pause to give others time to process the information.

- Let colleagues know they can ask questions to clarify their understanding without hesitation. In fact, encourage it. Ideally, you want them to feel confident enough to ask questions proactively before you need to address any potential confusion.

- Break down complex ideas into smaller, more manageable steps and explain the reasoning behind each step.

- To avoid getting impatient and interrupting, which I often still do, I take notes for myself during interactions. This not only keeps my mind busy but also keeps me present and focused in the moment. Additionally, it gives me a reason not to make eye contact for long periods of time.

Taking personal notes during conversations helps me stay engaged and avoid interrupting.

Respecting Different Working Styles

We were working on a routine project with fairly easy-to-meet goals. My entire team wanted to approach the project in their own manner, but I was convinced that my method, which was different from theirs, was the best way. I insisted that we follow my approach, which led to frustration among my team members. They felt stifled and unable to work in a way that suited their strengths. As a result, we didn't meet our goals, even though they were quite achievable, and it was a wake-up call for me. I realized that effective leadership means respecting different working styles.

Autistic individuals may develop highly efficient ways to complete tasks, but that doesn't mean others will—or should—follow the same methods. As autistic leaders, within reason, we need to give our teams the leeway to work in ways that best fit their needs.

- Recognize that your colleagues' different approaches to doing things are opportunities for you to learn from them.

- Focus on the goals, agree with the team on milestones along the way, and be less prescriptive about how to get there. Trust but verify. Allow team members the freedom to find their own ways to achieve goals as long as the desired outcomes are met.

- Adjust your expectations. This doesn't mean lowering your standards, but rather recognizing that not everyone will work at the same pace or in the same way you do. Set goals that are a stretch but attainable for your team.

A good leader values the team's approach, not just their own.

Communication

When I was in my twenties, I had a co-worker named Jerry—a smart person and someone I liked. He was always positive and quick to tell jokes. Unfortunately, I rarely understood those jokes because I took what he said literally. It got to the point where whenever he told a joke and I was nearby, he would hold up two fingers as a visual signal to me not to take what he said literally. It was confusing because I knew he was trying to be funny, but the humor was lost on me.

I couldn't help but think, "If you have to explain that it's a joke, is it really a joke?" I assumed I just didn't get his sense of humor, even though most people around me did.

When I became a leader, I thought of this example in reverse. I did my best to make sure my communication was clear and direct, recognizing that what might be obvious to one person could be completely misinterpreted by another.

Autistic individuals might struggle to interpret and convey ideas in ways that neurotypical colleagues expect, leading to misinterpretations and communication gaps. We may struggle with "reading between the lines"; indirect messages and non-verbal cues can be difficult to grasp, and we can often take things said literally.

- Where possible, encourage written over oral communication. This approach allows for the organization and clear presentation of ideas, as well as providing a record of agreements that can be referred to if needed. It is important to note, though, that documenting agreements is often a step used to manage individual performance problems. I let my team know upfront that this was merely how I communicated (and explicitly informed them when I was formally documenting a performance issue). Otherwise, team members might wrongly believe I was monitoring their performance or being overly critical, rather than ensuring clear communication.

- Use clear, direct language. Because autistic individuals may take language more literally, avoid using idioms, sarcasm, or figurative speech, which could easily be misconstrued.

- Check for understanding. After communicating important information, ask team members to paraphrase what they've heard or understood. This helps confirm that the message was received as intended and reduces the likelihood of future conflict.

A self-review before formal feedback creates space for employees to share their perspective and address any unspoken feedback you might not have picked up on.

Giving Performance Feedback

I finished giving performance reviews for my team and was feeling good. We had met our goals, and while there were areas for improvement, overall, the team performed well.

Later in the week, my boss asked to speak with me. He shared that it got back to him that I was harsh in my feedback of my team and that I focused only on what went wrong. I was surprised, as I thought I had positive conversations with my direct reports, only to find out later that they had a very different interpretation. I realized I needed to change my feedback methods to get my points across effectively.

Since then, I've adopted some strategies that help me to express my feedback in a way that keeps the needs of the recipient in mind.

- Use the "sandwich" method for feedback. This balanced approach—starting with positive feedback, providing constructive criticism, and ending with more positive feedback—makes it easier for the recipient to accept and act on the constructive points. This method is particularly helpful for me, as I'm naturally wired to notice things that are amiss and focus on problem-solving.

- Focus on results, not the person. Concentrate on specific actions that need adjustment rather than making it about the individual's character or personality. This makes the feedback feel less personal and more actionable.

- Maintain a neutral tone. Keep your tone calm and neutral to avoid emotional escalation. This helps keep the focus on the feedback itself, rather than on any perceived emotional intensity.

- In more formal environments, such as performance reviews, have a pre-step where you review the employee ahead of time in writing, and the employee also reviews themselves in writing. Hold a pre-review meeting where you each share what you've written. This gives the employee time to share things you might not have noticed or provide context for their performance before formalizing the review. While a good practice for neurotypicals, too, it's especially important for autistics because we may not pick up on subtle cues or unspoken feedback during an actual review.

Casually walking around the office gave me a natural way to build trust and learn from my team.

Fostering Personal Connections

When I started in my first leadership role, it didn't occur to me to share even simple, everyday personal details or to be involved with those of my team. I was focused on tasks and goals, and I assumed everyone else was, too. I also avoided asking my team about their lives, as I didn't want to pry.

Over time, I noticed they would stop talking when I entered a room and quickly shift the conversation to work-related topics. They didn't seem as engaged, and our interactions felt increasingly distanced. Then, I asked one team member how his daughter was doing. He responded that he was surprised I asked, as he didn't think I cared.

Ouch.

I did care, a lot, but I felt awkward initiating personal conversations and didn't want my awkwardness to make others feel uncomfortable. I wanted to build personal connections in a way that people would be receptive to and that wouldn't overwhelm me. So, I started out small and worked my way up.

Here are some ways to build personal connections at work:

- Walk around the office at regular times. Each morning, early afternoon, and late in the day as people are packing up to go home, do some laps around the room. Make an effort to acknowledge people on your rounds. Sometimes it can be just a nod, and other times you might stop to talk. People are often working on interesting things, and you can learn a lot. This approach helped me become more comfortable around others in a way that was easy for me (I didn't have to stop and talk; I could always keep going), and I think it made them more comfortable around me, too. An added benefit is that the act of walking served as a form of stimming, providing a calming and repetitive motion that helped me stay focused and grounded throughout the day.

- Keep a personal information spreadsheet on co-workers as a memory aid for meaningful conversations, ensuring they are used respectfully and kept private (don't be creepy). Some details to include could be the names of partners, kids, life milestones, and interests. Refer to this before interactions to personalize your conversations. While this can be a lot of work, I found that team members appreciated it when I remembered and asked about important events or people in their lives. The interest was genuine on my part, but I needed a system to be able to execute. The effort was well worth it.

- Acknowledge and celebrate significant milestones in your team members' lives. I used my personal spreadsheet to track various events and set up an email reminder system to alert me at the appropriate times. Depending on the type of event, I might send an all-team congratulatory email, have food brought in, or simply send a personal email or mention it individually during my daily laps. Again, my desire was genuine, but I needed tools to help me execute on that desire.

The Natalie Diggins User Manual

One of the most effective tools I created to work better with teammates is the Natalie Diggins User Manual (I work in tech, after all!). It's a sort of cheat sheet on how I operate. In it, I laid out how I communicated, my expectations, my working style, and my sensitivities. I couldn't expect my team to magically understand me, but I could try to better explain why I worked the way I did.

I then tested it with a few team members. Did everything make sense? Was it reasonable? Was I reasonable? How would they improve upon the document and our relationship? In turn, I asked them to create their own manuals so that I could better understand and support them.

A manual on how I work made my team more effective—and me more approachable.

Enhancing Neurodiverse Collaboration

So far, I've focused here on what autistics can do because that's what we can control. But what if I swapped the words autistic and neurotypical in my tactics above and reversed the perspective?

What if I were a neurotypical wanting to better understand neurodivergent individuals in the workplace? Just as I've made efforts to adapt and support my team, I hope neurotypicals would take the care and effort to understand and support their neurodivergent colleagues.

I come back to what I said earlier: While people on the spectrum may experience the world differently from neurotypicals, we still have many similarities. We all strive for understanding, respect, and the opportunity to contribute meaningfully to our roles.

Leadership, whether for autistic individuals or neurotypicals, is about continuous learning and adaptation. It's about recognizing and valuing the diversity of each individual, and adapting to meet the needs of our colleagues. It's about building a flexible toolkit that works for all of the people you lead.

⸬ **Tool:** Collaborative Leadership Questionnaire

While I created the Natalie Diggins User Manual to help my team work more effectively, you may not need to go to that level of effort by creating a formal document. Even without a manual, a good first step to understanding your leadership style is to reflect on these questions and use them to begin a meaningful conversation with team members.

Introduction

- **What is the purpose of creating this manual?**

How can this document support both me and my team by fostering a productive and collaborative working relationship?

Example:

I want our team to be effective and collaborative. To that end, this manual is meant to help you understand how I work, communicate, and lead. Rather than expect you to guess my leadership approach, the document is here to be a transparent guide. My hope is that it ensures we're aligned on expectations, communication, and collaboration.

_____

_____

_____

_____

- **What is your role, and how would you describe it to your team?**

How do I see my responsibilities in my role? What do I want my team to know about how I approach leadership?

_____

_____

_____

_____

Communication Style

- **How do you prefer to communicate?**

Do I prefer written or verbal communication? When do I find each style most effective?

_____

_____

_____

_____

- **What do you value in team communication?**

What qualities—like clarity, directness, or thoughtfulness—do I appreciate in how others communicate with me?

_____

_____

_____

_____

- **How do you prefer sensitive topics to be approached?**

When discussing sensitive issues, what approach helps me feel comfortable and prepared?

_____

_____

_____

_____

Decision-Making Style

- **How do you approach decisions?**

What steps do I take when making a decision? Do I rely on data, intuition, or a mix of both?

_____

_____

_____

_____

- **What information do I need to make decisions?**

What support, context, or information do I need from my team to make effective decisions?

_____

_____

_____

_____

- **What support do I value when faced with difficult choices?**

Consider what resources, feedback, or collaboration from your team can help you feel confident when faced with complex or challenging decisions.

_____

_____

_____

_____

Strengths: What the Team Can Rely on Me For

- **What do you excel at as a leader?**

What are my strongest leadership traits? How do they benefit my team and projects?

_____

_____

_____

- **What can your team rely on you for?**

When my team faces challenges, what strengths do I consistently bring to the table?

_____

_____

_____

_____

Areas Where You May Need Support

- **What might be challenging about working with you?**

What feedback have I gotten in the past, and how did I effectively address it?

_____

_____

_____

_____

- **How can your team help you succeed?**

What specific actions or feedback can my team provide to help me perform at my best?

_____

_____

_____

Expectations: Building a Collaborative Team Culture

- **What kind of team culture do you want to build?**

What values, behaviors, or attitudes do I want to foster in my team?

_____

_____

_____

_____

- **What do you expect from your team in daily interactions?**

How do I want my team to communicate, collaborate, and handle challenges?

_____

_____

_____

_____

How You Recharge and Manage Stress

- **What keeps you energized as a leader?**

What activities or work environments help me feel focused and motivated?

_____

_____

_____

- **What should your team avoid during stressful times?**

What kinds of actions or situations create additional stress for me, and how can my team help mitigate them?

_____

_____

_____

_____

Your Long-Term Goals for the Team

- **What are your aspirations for your team?**

How do I envision my team growing and achieving success over time?

_____

_____

_____

_____

- **How can your team provide feedback on your manual and leadership style?**

How do I want my team to approach me with ideas for improving our collaboration?

_____

_____

_____

_____

- **How can I learn how you work best?**

What are my employees' communication preferences, strengths, and areas where they may need support? What helps them feel most effective and comfortable in our collaboration? How can I help them be successful?

_____

_____

_____

_____

The Essentials:

Partnering with Your Doctor for Better Care

- Navigating healthcare with sensory sensitivities is about creating a partnership, not a struggle.

- Reflect on your sensory needs, communication preferences, and triggers before medical visits.

- Create a personalized medical communication letter to explain your needs clearly.

- Structure your letter with sections like noise, lighting, and physical contact preferences.

- Advocate for your comfort without hesitation—your experience is your expertise.

Partnering with Your Doctor for Better Care

I hadn't even seen the doctor and I was already on edge.

I checked myself in online on the medical group's web portal to avoid unnecessary human contact. When I arrived, the clinic's waiting area was blessedly uncrowded. So far, so good. However, the overhead fluorescent lighting in the exam room glared. Should I put on my sunglasses?

I removed my earplugs to be fully present, but there was a lot of background noise coming at me at once: the rattle from the air conditioner, people talking loudly nearby, and then someone, just outside my exam room, dropped a heavy box on the ground. Wait, is that a bouncing screensaver on the computer next to me? Look away!

I told myself, I can do this, I can do this, I can do this.

Loud noises, bright lights, crowded spaces, and background movement can all be overwhelming to me. I was about to have my first significant medical procedure, and I didn't know what to expect. How was I going to get through the experience?

Navigating the healthcare system can be challenging for anyone, but especially for those of us with ASD. We all experience the world in different ways, and our sensory sensitivities, communication styles, and coping mechanisms can vary widely.

That's why effective communication with healthcare providers is crucial for ensuring we receive the best possible care with minimal distress. A personalized medical communication letter can be a valuable tool to help convey your needs and preferences clearly. By creating one, you can provide your healthcare team with the information they need to accommodate your specific needs.

A personalized medical communication letter is a tool that bridges understanding between you and your doctor.

When I shared my own letter with my doctor, she was surprised initially, and then she became curious. She admitted she hadn't had a patient like me before (although she probably did but didn't know it) and wanted to learn more. We were able to work together to make the experience more manageable for both of us.

Since then, I've shared my form with several doctors. Most recently, one told me she wasn't surprised at all. It was heartening to hear that more doctors are now being trained to support neurodivergent patients—and that she had been through that training herself.

Below is a step-by-step guide to help you craft your own letter, plus mine as an example. This is only meant as a starting point, and I encourage you to improve upon my version to create something that works for you.

Understand Your Needs

Start by reflecting on your personal sensitivities and preferences in medical settings. Consider how sensory issues, anxiety triggers, and communication styles affect your healthcare experience. Identifying these factors will help you clearly articulate your needs.

Organize Key Information

Organize your thoughts by creating sections for different types of information. Using bullet points or numbered lists can enhance clarity and readability. Each section should address a specific aspect of your experience that you want your healthcare provider to understand.

The more specific your letter is, the more it equips your doctor to provide better care.

Write Your Letter

Begin with a brief introduction about yourself and your diagnosis. This sets the context for the healthcare provider and underscores the importance of understanding your needs. Some specific areas for consideration:

- **Noise Sensitivity:** Explain how noise affects you and share any tools you use, such as earplugs. Are there things your doctor can do to make you more comfortable?

- **Crowded Spaces:** Mention your anxiety in crowded spaces and request advice on less busy times for appointments. Politely ask that only essential personnel be present during your appointments.

- **Lighting Sensitivity:** Discuss your sensitivity to lighting and mention if you might wear sunglasses. Request adjustable lighting if possible.

- **Movement Sensitivity:** Explain your sensitivity to movement and request minimal unnecessary movement around you.

- **Physical Contact:** State your preference for physical contact and ask for explanations of procedures beforehand.

- **Additional Requests:** Mention any need for detailed explanations of medical procedures. If you value understanding processes and outcomes, this can help you feel informed and at ease.

Encourage Open Communication

Invite your healthcare provider to ask questions about your condition or accommodations. Emphasize that their understanding will greatly improve your comfort and care.

Advocating for your needs is empowering, but not every provider will have the resources to meet every request. Still, asking ensures that your needs are understood and considered. Even small accommodations—such as adjusting lighting or explaining steps beforehand—can make a significant difference in your experience.

While not universal, today many healthcare professionals have training on how to best support neurodivergent people, but in my own experience, they've had limited practical exposure. By opening a dialogue and sharing your needs, you not only help yourself but also contribute to their learning and ability to support future patients with similar needs.

Doctors are learning, but you are the expert on your experience.

Create a Partnership

By advocating for your needs and fostering a partnership, you can shift healthcare from something to endure into something that truly supports you. Clarity and communication don't just make your care better—they help shape a system that works for all neurodivergent patients.

With gratitude to Dr. Nicole Alicino.

⠿ **Tool:** Example Medical Letter

By clearly articulating specific sensitivities, preferences, and requests up-front, you provide your doctor with the tools to create a more comfortable and supportive medical experience. Use my medical letter as an example to craft your own, and remember to update it as your needs evolve or based on feedback from healthcare providers.

Dear Doctor,

I am reaching out to share some information about my health that may affect my medical care. Although I typically operate with high executive function and may appear neurotypical, I have been formally diagnosed with Autism Spectrum Disorder (ASD) Level 1 and alexithymia, according to the DSM-5 criteria.

Understanding my condition is crucial, especially as it might affect my inter-actions in a medical environment. Here are key points that could influence my comfort and response during medical treatment:

- **Noise Sensitivity:** Sudden or loud noises are very distressing for me. If possible, please ensure a quiet environment during our appointments. Minimizing noise from medical equipment and conversations can help reduce my anxiety. I tend to wear earplugs in particularly noisy environ-ments, and I may do so during our appointments.

- **Crowded Spaces:** I experience anxiety in crowded spaces. For this rea-son, where possible I schedule appointments during less busy times. Additionally, I would feel more comfortable if only essential personnel are present in the room during my appointments. While I understand the importance of medical training, I kindly request not to be examined by others for training purposes.

- **Lighting Sensitivity:** Intense lighting can be overwhelming. If the lighting in the examination room is adjustable, please consider dimming it to a more comfortable level for me, assuming it doesn't adversely impact medical treatment. When it is not possible to adjust the lighting, please do not be surprised if I opt to wear sunglasses to manage the sensitivity.

- **Movement Sensitivity:** I am quite sensitive to the movement of people and objects around me. Minimizing unnecessary movement in my vicinity can help me stay calm.

- **Physical Contact:** I prefer to avoid physical contact when it is not necessary. Please explain any physical examinations or procedures beforehand.

Additionally, I might ask for detailed explanations during our interactions. As a technologist, understanding procedures and anticipated outcomes is vital for me. Providing thorough explanations can help me feel more at ease and better comprehend what to expect.

Please feel free to ask me any questions about my condition or any specific accommodations that could help. Your consideration of these elements will greatly improve my comfort and the quality of care I receive.

Thank you for taking these elements into consideration as we work together to manage my health.

Warm Regards,

The Essentials:

Creating an Autistic-Friendly Jury Duty Experience

- People with autism aren't automatically disqualified from serving on a jury and can bring valuable perspectives.

- Options for support include requesting accommodations, having private discussions with judges, or seeking exemptions.

- Environmental adjustments like quieter courtrooms and pre-trial visits can reduce sensory overload.

- Prioritize accommodations that enable you to participate fully and confidently.

- Your viewpoint matters—it adds depth and diversity to the judicial process.

Creating an Autistic-Friendly Jury Duty Experience

I was called for jury duty again, but this time it was different—I made it all the way through to the jury selection process. The stakes were much higher, with the trial expected to last for months, and the massive, imposing court chamber looked like a C-SPAN hearing on Capitol Hill, filled with people moving about.

As part of the jury empanelment process, I sat in the courtroom awaiting my turn, my anxiety growing. Finally, my name was called, and I was sworn in.

Defense lawyer: *Have you or anyone close to you ever been the victim of a violent crime?*

My mind and its need for accuracy went into action. How did the court define violent crime? What if people close to me had been victims, but I didn't know? I myself had been a victim, but I didn't press charges. Could I claim I was a victim if I had no legal proof?

The exchange became testy as I asked increasingly detailed clarifying questions, which were likely misinterpreted as me being difficult and trying to get out of jury duty. I was sternly admonished by the judge.

Then I panicked. No one in the room knew I was autistic. *How did it get to this point? Would I be sent to jail?*

I wish I knew then what I know now. Since then, I've learned how important it is to know what options and accommodations are available for autistic individuals in the jury process. I'm hoping that what I learned could help others serve with less stress and more confidence.

Being autistic doesn't automatically disqualify someone from serving on a jury (nor do I believe it should). Jurors must be able to understand and retain information, follow courtroom procedures, evaluate evidence impartially, reason logically, engage in deliberations with other jurors, and sit through the entire trial without disruption. Fitness to serve is determined on a case-by-case basis.

Being autistic doesn't mean you can't serve; it means you may serve differently.

In addition to these technical requirements, people on the spectrum may face added challenges due to the ways our brains are wired. We may face challenges with sensory processing, social interactions, and communication. These differences can make the jury duty experience even more demanding, to the point of experiencing significant physical and mental distress.

Each jurisdiction is different, but where I live now, I have at least three alternatives: request an accommodation, request a private conversation with the trial judge, and request to be excused.

Request an Accommodation

Not all autistic individuals experience the same challenges or have the same support needs. Perhaps you feel that you can serve jury duty if certain accommodations are made. Reach out in advance of your service to the local office responsible for your jury selection and share your situation.

The more specific you can be about your needs, the more the court system can assist you. Keep in mind that accommodations are your right under the Americans with Disabilities Act (ADA), ensuring equal access and inclusion in the jury process. While courts try to provide reasonable accommodations, some limitations may exist due to the nature of legal proceedings or available resources.

Your needs matter, and the court is there to support you when you express them clearly.

Accommodations vary widely and can be tailored to meet individual needs, whether someone requires a sensory-friendly environment, assistance with communication, or support navigating the legal process. Some accommodations to consider:

Environmental Adjustments

- **Pre-Trial Visit:** Arrange a pre-trial visit to the courtroom to become familiar with the environment and reduce anxiety. Ask for an orientation session with court personnel to explain the jury process, roles of courtroom participants, and what to expect during the trial. I have been called to serve twice at the same location and found it comforting to already know where everything is located. Additionally, the clerk responsible for your jury pool will review court procedures on the day of jury selection. So, if you're still unsure about certain specifics after the tour, you'll have another chance to hear many of the same things again when you report for duty.

- **Sensory-Friendly Environment:** Ask for a quieter courtroom, permission to use noise-canceling headphones, or a seating arrangement away from bright lights and excessive noise.
- **Break Room:** Request access to a quiet room for breaks to decompress from sensory overload or stress.

Scheduling Flexibility

- **Clear Schedules:** Request a detailed schedule of daily proceedings to help manage expectations. Each court is different, but they all operate with their own set schedule.
- **Modified Schedule:** Ask for shorter or more frequent breaks to manage sensory overload or fatigue.

Communication Support

- **Clear Communication:** Request written instructions and direct communication from the judge and attorneys.
- **Guided Advocacy:** Ask for access to a court liaison or advocate to help communicate needs effectively.
- **Alternative Reporting Methods:** Allow responses or questions to be submitted in writing if verbal communication is challenging.

Assistive Support

- **Documentation Support:** Ask to be allowed a support person to help with filling out forms or processing information.
- **Assistive Technology:** Seek permission to use devices such as laptops or tablets for notetaking or accessing assistive communication tools (e.g., speech-to-text apps for verbal responses or noise-canceling devices for managing sensory challenges), where permitted by courtroom rules.

- **Support Person:** Request a support person or advocate to be present during the trial for communication or emotional support.

Physical Comfort

- **Flexible Seating:** Request the ability to move or stand periodically to reduce physical discomfort or restlessness.

In my experience, court personnel were eager to help and appreciated the opportunity to learn more about accommodating individuals with autism. By being proactive and clear about your needs, you can also help create a more inclusive and understanding judicial system.

Request a Private Discussion with the Trial Judge

Ideally, if you've reached the jury selection process and require accommodations, you've already requested them in advance. Even so, you may encounter unanticipated situations or realize that, despite your accommodations, you need additional support or you find yourself unable to continue.

The good news is that during the jury selection process, the judge will usually give jurors the chance to speak privately if they have personal concerns. This is your opportunity to communicate any issues you're facing.

Judges are there to ensure fairness—
don't hesitate to speak privately if needed.

During one jury selection process, I realized that I couldn't serve, no matter the accommodations. I took the judge up on his offer of a private consultation, and I received nothing but understanding and respect.

If the judge does not offer this opportunity, you can request to speak privately.

Request to Be Excused

If you feel that you need an exemption from service, districts generally recommend making your request in advance and including some form of the following information:

- Email subject or first line of letter: ADA Accommodation Request
- Your name
- A brief description of your disability and why you feel you can't serve
- Name of the case (and number, if known)
- Name of the judge (if known)
- Date(s) you will be in court
- Your contact information, including mailing address, email address, and phone number

One district suggested I obtain a letter from my doctor stating why I was unable to serve. Another suggested I simply call their office. Each court has different procedures, so these are merely examples. Start by contacting the office responsible for jury selection in your community. Reach out early so there is enough time to process your request.

Remember, the goal is to ensure you can serve effectively and comfortably.

Ultimately, the decision to serve or seek an exemption is a deeply personal one, and it depends on your individual needs and circumstances. While some—wrongly—question an autistic's ability to serve on a jury, I believe that we bring a wide range of valuable strengths and perspectives to the jury process. With the right support and accommodations, autistic individuals can not only fulfill this duty but excel in it.

The right to a fair trial includes the right to a jury that reflects all of society.

Serving on a jury is a civic duty that reflects the diversity and complexity of our society. A jury pool is intended to be a representation of that diversity. If our perspectives aren't included, we miss out on having a voice in that society.

Just as we give by serving, we gain by helping create the sort of world we want to live in.

With gratitude to the Honorable Ramona A. Gonzalez.

Tool: Jury Duty Preparation Checklist

Preparing for jury duty and knowing what to expect can help you feel more confident and in control. This checklist is designed to guide you through each step of the process, recognizing that your needs may vary, and additional steps might be necessary. Planning ahead and addressing potential challenges can make the experience smoother and less stressful.

Before Jury Duty:

○ Research your local court's accommodations policies.

○ Contact the jury pool clerk to request accommodations in advance, if needed.

○ Schedule a pre-trial visit to the courthouse.

○ Prepare a sensory toolkit (noise-canceling headphones, comfort items, etc.).

○ Ensure that all sensory aids comply with courtroom rules.

○ Obtain a detailed schedule of proceedings, if available.

○ Prepare a brief statement to explain your accommodation needs if asked.

○ Arrange transportation to ensure a smooth arrival.

Day of Jury Duty:

○ Bring all necessary documentation (summons, ID).

○ Pack essentials: snacks, water, and sensory aids.

○ Locate quiet spaces for breaks during downtime.

○ Request breaks as needed for sensory or emotional challenges.

If Challenges Arise:

○ Request a private conversation with the judge to address concerns.

○ Communicate if you need additional breaks or adjustments.

○ Speak to court personnel if clarification or further assistance is needed.

After Jury Duty:

○ Allow time to decompress and recharge after the experience.

○ Reflect on what worked well and what could be improved for next time.

Adapting Strategies to Fit AuDHD Needs

I once had an autistic co-worker with ADHD tell me, "It feels like I have two operating systems—one that needs routine and another that struggles to follow it." That stuck with me. If you're autistic and also have ADHD—sometimes called AuDHD—you might recognize that tension between needing structure and finding it hard to maintain.

This push and pull can make it challenging to find strategies that actually work.

It's not uncommon for someone with autism to also have ADHD, so you might wonder why I didn't directly address AuDHD in this guide. While I want to be helpful on this important subject, it's not part of my lived experience. Thus, I don't feel qualified to do so.

That said, if you do have AuDHD, it's my hope that many of these ideas and tools may still work for you, or that they'll work for you with modifications.

For example:

- In the **"How to Build a Sensory Diet That Keeps You Balanced"** chapter, I suggest keeping a sensory journal. If staying consistent is difficult, try setting **timed reminders on your phone** to check in on your sensory needs throughout the day. You might also **pair these check-ins with existing habits**—such as before meals, during breaks, or after finishing a specific task—to build a routine.

- In the **"Building Friendships That Work for You (and Your Friends)"** chapter, I emphasize the importance of consistency and checking in with friends. If remembering to check in is a challenge, **automating the process** might help. Apps like Google Messages, iMessage, and WhatsApp allow you to schedule messages in advance. You can write a message when you think of it—or even draft several at once—then schedule them to send at different times, pacing yourself while staying connected.

- In the **"Setting Yourself Up for Social Gatherings"** chapter, I suggest using a matrix to decide whether to attend an event. If a matrix feels overwhelming or difficult to follow, a more **visual, color-coded chart** might make it easier to use.

- In the **"Masking, Unmasking, and Finding Balance"** chapter, I suggest paying attention to how you're feeling during unmasking experiments. If self-reflection is hard to retain, **recording quick voice memos** or **jotting down notes** in the moment could be useful to reference later.

- In the **"Partnering with Your Doctor for Better Care"** chapter, I suggest creating a personalized medical communication letter to clearly convey your needs and preferences. But that's just one part of building a two-way partnership with your doctors. If they give too much information at once, you can ask them to **summarize key points at the end of the appointment** and **request written instructions** for later review.

These are just a few examples—your needs may be different. If so, how might you create modifications on your own that work specifically for you?

Customizing Strategies for AuDHD

First, identify what's holding you back from successfully using these tools. What feels difficult or overwhelming?

Then, ask yourself:

- Can I make it more visual? (e.g., turning lists into color-coded charts)
- Can I break it into smaller steps? (e.g., setting step-by-step reminders)
- Can I use technology to support me? (e.g., using voice memos or scheduling messages in advance)

Once you find what works best for you, ask yourself:

- Can I tie any of these modifications to an existing routine that I'm already comfortable with?

New strategies stick better when they're linked to something familiar. Instead of building habits from scratch, try layering them onto routines you already do—like checking your sensory needs when you brush your teeth, setting reminders when you prepare meals, or scheduling check-ins while reviewing your calendar. The easier it is to integrate, the more likely it is to become second nature.

Some strategies will need adjusting depending on your energy, focus, or executive function that day. The key is flexibility: having multiple ways to approach a task so you can adapt when needed.

The goal isn't perfection; it's progress—finding what works for you and refining it over time.

Glossary

These definitions are meant to reflect the author's practical and lived experiences rather than being exhaustive technical definitions.

Accommodations

Adjustments that help autistic individuals navigate environments, tasks, or interactions by reducing barriers and improving accessibility.

Alexithymia

A condition where it's difficult to identify or describe your own emotions or others'. It's like feeling emotions but struggling to label or express them.

Americans with Disabilities Act (ADA)

A law protecting people with disabilities from discrimination in work, education, and public life. It promotes equal access and opportunities for all.

Applied Behavioral Analysis (ABA)

A therapy using reinforcement techniques to modify behaviors. Its use in autism treatment is controversial due to differing views on its goals and impact.

Associative Thinking

The ability to connect ideas that might seem unrelated. It's a creative process that links concepts through personal experiences or patterns.

Attention-Deficit/Hyperactivity Disorder (ADHD)

A condition affecting focus, self-control, and behavior. It often involves difficulty paying attention, staying still, or managing impulses.

Autonomic Response

The body's automatic reaction to stress or stimuli, such as increased heart rate or sweating. These responses occur without conscious control.

Autism and Attention-Deficit/Hyperactivity Disorder (AuDHD)

A term for individuals who are both autistic and have ADHD. It combines traits from both conditions, such as a need for structure with difficulty maintaining it, or sensory sensitivity with impulsivity.

Autism Spectrum Disorder (ASD)

A developmental condition affecting communication, behavior, and sensory experiences. It's called a "spectrum" because it presents differently in each person, ranging from mild to more significant characteristics.

Autism Spectrum Disorder Levels

For individuals on the autism spectrum, this refers to the level of support needed for social communication, daily living, and emotional regulation, ranging from Level 1 (requiring minimal support) to Level 3 (requiring substantial support).

Autistic

A term for someone with autism, a condition affecting communication, behavior, and sensory experiences. Autism varies greatly from person to person.

Autistic Burnout

A state of intense exhaustion and overwhelm from prolonged stress, social demands, or sensory overload. It significantly impacts an autistic person's ability to cope with daily life.

Bridezilla

A term for a bride who becomes overly stressed or demanding during wedding planning. Often used humorously, it can reflect pressure-related anxiety.

C-SPAN

A U.S.-based television network that provides unfiltered, live coverage of political events, including congressional hearings, debates, and public affairs programming.

Diagnostic and Statistical Manual (DSM)

A manual used by professionals to diagnose mental health conditions, including autism. It standardizes how conditions are identified and understood. As of this writing, the current edition is the fifth, referred to as DSM-5.

Double Empathy Problem

Describes the mutual difficulty neurotypical and neurodivergent people face in understanding each other's unique experiences and emotions, often causing misunderstandings.

Executive Function

Cognitive skills that help with planning, organization, decision-making, and task management. Challenges in this area can affect time management, flexibility, and impulse control.

FOMO (Fear of Missing Out)

Anxiety or concern about missing out on social events or experiences, often heightened by others sharing them online or in person.

Haptic Gloves

Wearable gloves that simulate touch by providing physical feedback. Used in virtual reality, gaming, and sensory therapy.

High-Fidelity Earplugs

Earplugs designed to reduce overall sound levels while maintaining the clarity of music and speech. Ideal for concerts or performances.

Hyper-Connected Sensory Processing

Heightened sensitivity to sights, sounds, smells, or touch, leading to increased awareness. It can sometimes feel overwhelming.

Hyperfocus and Awareness

Intense and sometimes involuntary focus on a task or interest, which may cause a loss of time awareness or surroundings. Common among some neurodivergent individuals.

Introversion

A personality trait where someone feels recharged by alone time rather than social interaction.

Introvert

A person who feels recharged by alone time rather than social interaction.

Masking

Unconsciously or consciously hiding autistic traits to fit social norms. It can help with social acceptance but often leads to exhaustion and loss of self-identity.

Meltdowns

A full-body response to overwhelm, triggered by stress or sensory overload. It may look like an outburst or loss of control, but unlike tantrums, it is involuntary and not goal-driven. Recovery time is often needed.

Neurodevelopmental Condition

Conditions affecting brain and nervous system development, like autism or ADHD. They can impact learning, behavior, and communication.

Neurodivergent (ND)

Refers to people whose brain functions differ from societal norms for "typical." Includes autism, ADHD, dyslexia, and similar conditions.

Neurotype

A term for how an individual's brain processes information, whether neurodivergent or neurotypical.

Neurotypical (NT)

Describes people whose brain functions align with societal norms for "typical."

Olivia Rodrigo

A Grammy-winning singer-songwriter known for her emotionally charged lyrics and genre-blending music. Her music often reflects personal experiences, creating a genuine connection with her audience.

Parallel Processing

Handling multiple streams of information at once. Observed in some neuro-divergent individuals, it enables thinking and responding to multiple things simultaneously, though experiences vary.

People Hangover

Exhaustion after socializing, common for introverts or neurodivergent people who find interactions draining.

Sensory Diet

A personalized routine to manage sensory input for focus, comfort, and regulation. It involves making intentional choices about environments, activities, and tools to balance stimulation and prevent overwhelm.

Sensory Overload

Overwhelm caused by excessive sensory inputs like bright lights, loud noises, or strong smells. It may lead to stress, anxiety, or, in autistic people, meltdowns or shutdowns.

Shutdowns

A response to overwhelm where a person shuts down mentally or physically, becoming unresponsive or detached.

Sound-Adaptive Earplugs

Earplugs that automatically adjust to changing noise levels, reducing disruptive background noise while allowing important sounds, like speech, to come through clearly.

Stimming

Repetitive movements or sounds that help regulate sensory input and emotions. Common in people with autism, examples include hand-flapping, rocking, or humming.

Vocal Stimming

A type of stimming involving vocal sounds like humming, repeating words, or making noise to help manage emotions or sensory overload.

With Appreciation

The journalist David Brooks once said that writers write to learn what they need to learn. That's certainly true for me. I'm grateful to have worked on this project so that I could fine-tune my own tools. Each chapter became a form of deep introspection and, in many ways, intensive therapy. I'm in a much better place as a result.

Thank you to Dr. Nicole Alicino, Dr. Naomi Bravmann, and Dr. Natalie Engelbrecht for seeing and supporting me. Each of you offered something I needed, right when I needed it—even when I couldn't yet name what that was.

A special thank you to Dr. Alicino, who also read an early draft and offered thoughtful, nuanced feedback. Her questions and reflections helped me strengthen the manuscript and deepen my thinking about how it could support the reader. I'm also grateful to the other early readers who chose to remain unnamed but gave their time and perspectives as the manuscript took shape.

Warm thanks to Robin Schroffel for her thoughtful eye and care with the language. Her work helped make this book stronger and more readable.

The Honorable Ramona A. Gonzalez offered invaluable input on the jury duty chapter. Her commitment to justice—and to increasing autistic participation in the legal system—is inspiring.

And thank you to my husband, my first reader and editor, who gave me the space and grace to write this book. Yes, I'm a double shot of espresso, but you're still a strong cup of coffee.

To every autistic adult navigating a world not built for us: I see you.

About the Author

Natalie Diggins is a technologist, board member, and angel investor with a career built on solving complex system problems and scaling emerging technologies. Diagnosed with autism and alexithymia as an adult, she spent years searching for practical tools to navigate a neurotypical world—only to discover that many simply didn't exist. So, she built them. Drawing from both her analytical mindset and lived experience, she now shares the real-world tools she wishes had been available—simple, approachable frameworks designed to help autistic adults thrive.

She lives in New York City with her husband.

Index

C

D

E

F

M

T

www.ingramcontent.com/pod-product-compliance
Lightning Source LLC
Chambersburg PA
CBHW060136130626
46556CB00006B/2365